The pergola in the garden at Notre Dame de Vie, Picasso's last house.
Above, Jacqueline with her daughter, Cathy, in August 1966.

*L'Homme au Mouton,* the only Picasso sculpture in the garden. It
stands just a few steps from the sculpture room where the other
Picasso pieces are displayed. Another cast of this famous work
stands in a square in Vallauris; the third is at the Museum of
Modern Art in New York.

Left: The patio at the entrance to Notre Dame de Vie. At the left is Jacqueline's little house.

Below: Picasso is going for a drive on this beautiful June day in 1966. The car is an ancient Hispano Suiza, vintage 1933.

# Forever Picasso

# Forever

# Roberto Otero

*translated by Elaine Kerrigan*

# Picasso

*An Intimate Look at*
*His Last Years*

Harry N. Abrams Inc., Publishers, N.Y.

To Jacqueline, who shared and helped make possible these last years.

Edited by Margaret L. Kaplan

Library of Congress Cataloging in Publication Data

Otero, Roberto.
  Forever Picasso:  an intimate look at his last years.

  1.  Picasso, Pablo, 1881–1973.  I  Title.
ND553.P507413      759.4      74–2304
ISBN 0–8109–0369–5

Library of Congress Catalogue Card Number: 74–2304
Printed and bound in Italy

# INTRODUCTION

Several versions exist of how the author of this book came to meet Pablo Picasso: They met by chance on the beach at Cannes while Picasso was drawing in the sand...; with Daniel Zarza, a gypsy from Huelva, singing *burlerias*...; with Rafaël Alberti and his daughter Aitana, indulging in a tasty snack of chorizo, on a May afternoon...; with Tota Cuevas and La Hormiguita del Carril, close friends of Picasso, during a masked ball at the Baron de Rothschild's...; with César Cecci, doctor, musician, poet, and all-around Mad Hatter, born in Santiago de Chile, an intimate of Thomas Mann and Salvador Allende, and, what is more, the nephew of a famous Italian antarctic explorer who was eaten alive by some famished colleagues...; with Max Jacob and Casagemas at a discreet but intimate banquet featuring a sumptuous stew of jugged hare prepared by Jacqueline (a memorable evening during which Picasso discussed black art and an anarchist bank robbery in Barcelona with Casagemas and which he recalled for years, for several months afterward awakening his wife at three in the morning to remind her of the occasion and talk about it till dawn)...; at the Anchorenas' in Paris during World War II, as suckling pig, roasted skin and all, was eaten in the style of Argentine gauchos on the pampas....

Little—perhaps nothing—is known about Roberto Otero, except that he has to his credit several hefty dossiers filed in one or another intelligence bureau. It seems he did go to kindergarten, spent some time as student, poet, prose writer, filmmaker, publisher, trafficker in arms, glider pilot, photographer, and secretary to a now deposed tyrant. At the moment he is a solitary sailor. He lives quite happily on his yacht based in the Mediterranean. The boat is 38 feet long, boasts sails, a steel hull, and a 350-horsepower Mercedes-Benz motor. It was constructed in Holland. He occasionally dreams of selling it for a fair price to raise funds quickly to finance a film venture in the Antilles.

The reader will see for himself as he notes the evident interdependence of text and photographs that this book could have been a film documentary. It was actually conceived as such, and the facts are as follows: In 1964, Otero had just finished making three full-length documentaries. The subject of the first was the Spanish poet Federico García Lorca; the second film was on General Perón in exile; the third dealt with novice bullfighters in Spain. This last subject of bulls and bullfighters was a matter of passionate interest to both Picasso and Otero. They spent entire days talking bulls, mingling their own special blend of dead seriousness and riotous horseplay. For Picasso, the founder of Cubism, as well as other mighty trends, that blend was indispensable.

One afternoon the author of this book suggested to Picasso that he, Roberto Otero, make a documentary on him—his life at Notre Dame de Vie and various aspects of his work. Otero proposed to emphasize the contrast between the idyllic life Picasso led with Jacqueline Roque and her daughter Cathy and the senseless frustration he suffered as a revolutionary painter faced with total lack of understanding on the part of the French Communist Party's cultural bureaucracy. He also had it in mind to emphasize the growing element of eroticism in Picasso's late work. Picasso agreed, naturally, but the film never materialized. It was always in the process of being "half made." The ostensible reasons were two, but the real reason was one, and one alone. As for the ostensible reasons, Picasso objected to having a film company shooting in his house, recalling that when Clouzot had been there, "he had made life impossible because he moved everything around to where it didn't belong" (an obvious pretext, considering the "organized disorder" that prevailed in the Picasso household). The second so-called reason was revealed every time the subject was broached, and that was daily, especially during the summer when the painter and the author were together. Picasso would procrastinate, saying, "We're still young, aren't we? There's more than enough time for that." The real reason was that Roberto Otero did not have a cent to his name. Regularly, after dinner, as he bade his friend Picasso goodnight, the master would say, "But why in the world don't you do it by yourself? The same as the photos." And that is how Otero recollects that incredible summer.

One fine day Otero discovered that he had taken some two thousand photographs of Picasso and had accumulated twenty-eight notebooks of conversations of the kid from Málaga and his cuadrilla, on endless topics. It suddenly struck him that he could write a book as if it were a documentary film, imagining the text as the voice of the invisible narrator.

And that is the background of the book you are about to read and of its author. Like Picasso's own art, some of it is distorted, some merely capricious. But as in any art work—and surely Otero himself is as much a work of art as his book—there is a core of truth to be discovered here. This discovery will be the reader's pleasure.

ELAINE KERRIGAN

# Contents

# Part I

# HAPPENINGS

Picasso with Edward Steichen, a friend for some sixty years. It was Steichen who organized Picasso's first New York exhibition, at the Photo-Secession Gallery, in 1911.

# CHAPTER 1

# A Telegram from an Old Friend

I am downstairs in the living room at Notre Dame de Vie, reading a book Picasso has lent me. A slight stir of footsteps tells me he has awakened from his siesta and is on the first floor. The sound of his steps disappears down the long corridor which leads from the tiny entrance of the house to the kitchen. He is surely in search of Jacqueline. He does the same every day upon awakening. I am absorbed in reading the delightful *Memoirs of Manolo*. (Manolo Hugué was a Catalan sculptor and the quintessential bohemian artist of the turn of the century. Picasso tells thousands of tales in which his friend Manolo plays the purest and most ineffable of picaresque roles. "He tells a lot of fibs," Picasso told me when he gave me the book, "but it doesn't make it any the less amusing.") Suddenly the sound of the bells which hang at the door to the corridor rouses me from that distant summer in Ceret described by Manolo at the beginning of the century. I raise my eyes without lowering the book. Picasso puts his head through the frame of the half-open door with the air of a naughty child.

"Are you alone?" he asks.

"Yes."

"Where are the women?"

"I don't know. Perhaps upstairs in Catherine's room." (Catherine is Jacqueline's daughter.)

He sits down at my side in his favorite barber-style swivel chair and spins about several times absent-mindedly. He has momentarily forgotten his search for Jacqueline. Putting his hand in one of his pockets, he pulls out a telegram folded neatly in four.

"Read this," he says, "it's from an old friend."

The telegram reads more or less like this:

"DEAR PABLO, I HOPE YOU REMEMBER ME. I AM IN ANTIBES AT THE HOUSE OF FRIENDS. I WOULD LIKE TO SEE YOU. I WILL TELEPHONE TOMORROW. EDWARD STEICHEN."

"Do you know who Steichen is?" he asks.

"The photographer, isn't he?"

"No."

"Then I don't know who he is."

"Well, yes and no, like everything. For you he's a photographer and for me he's the person who took my first exhibition of drawings to the U.S." And, as I cannot conceal my surprise, he goes on: "He didn't manage to sell a thing."

6 August 1966

There is some unusual bustling about in the living room. Not only are Steichen and his wife there, but Jacqueline has taken advantage of the occasion to invite two friends who for several months have been discreetly awaiting the end of Picasso's convalescence: Douglas Cooper, the English art critic, and Justin Thannhauser, the New York collector and son of the dealer who gave Picasso his first show in Germany a half century before. Another couple has come along with the Steichens. The husband is a small, active, smiling man who introduces himself as Joseph Hirshhorn. Picasso excitedly comments that he has just discovered we are in the presence of "one of the biggest collectors in America and probably the world."

The guests are still standing. Picasso, moved by Steichen's presence, is transfixed and stares lingeringly into Steichen's eyes. Steichen is no less moved than Picasso. They smile at each other without knowing what to say. I regret not having a camera within reach so that I could catch that moment before everything changes, before they become used to seeing one another again.

Visibly upset, Picasso starts talking to me in Spanish while

Edward Steichen and his wife, Joanna, with Picasso in the sculpture room.

The sculpture room at Notre Dame de Vie.

continuing to glance back at Steichen, who goes on smiling with pent-up emotion though he does not understand a word. The monologue lasts a couple of minutes, until I also begin to share the general unease and awkwardness of the guests. I decide to interrupt him somehow, since I know he can go on talking this way in Spanish for a good while. The moment comes when he tells me, once more, that this is none other than the Steichen who brought his first drawings to the U.S. and did not manage to sell a one.

"I'd like to remind him of it," I interrupt, and then briefly recapitulate the last part of the soliloquy for Steichen.

"That's not quite exact," the photographer answers slowly, with deliberation. "We sold three. Do you remember, Pablo? Three."

"Ah yes, that's right," Picasso agrees. "He sold three, only three."

And we all laugh, somewhat relieved.

The ice is only partially broken, however. While I exchange a few words with Hirshhorn, I watch Picasso out of the corner of my eye and realize he is still shaken by the emotion of the encounter. Just then Jacqueline comes in carrying a tray of drinks, and when everyone turns toward her, Picasso seizes the moment to disappear through the door that leads to his studio. As is usual with him—especially when guests do not speak either Spanish or French fluently, as in this case—he has not been able to tolerate the lack of communication and has gone to look for some sort of exotic object with which to entertain everyone. It would not be at all strange to see him return in a few minutes wearing a red fur hat or ringing a huge sheep's bell, a gift from Spain, much to the astonishment or hilarity of the newly arrived guests. Before closing the door he sees me looking at him and asks me to follow.

The floor of the studio is strewn with the most unlikely and outlandish objects: piles of newspapers, books, engravings; an unfinished model for a sculpture for Chicago; pots of paint, brushes, copper plates, lamps, bits of string, wire, flattened tubes, spatulas, penknives, and so on. The strange thing about this enormous room is that there are no paintings in it except for Miró's self-portrait, barely visible in a half-dark, distant corner. It is propped on the only easel in the room.

Picasso is searching for something in the jumbled mountain of objects piled on a narrow table against the back wall of the studio. Suddenly he stops, his hands at his waist with palms forward and thumbs back, in a very characteristic gesture, and says:

"But do you know who Steichen is?"

It seems he is determined to tease.

"Of course I do. You've already told me several times and you have just finished telling everybody else. He's the person who took your first exhibition of drawings to the States."

"No, no! He's a very important photographer. The best photographer in America. One of the fathers of modern photography."

If one did not know his usual style of carrying on a conversation, it would be impossible to tell whether he is joking or just beginning to talk seriously.

"An incredible person, Steichen. Imagine, he photographed his wife—not this one with him now, but another—as if she were a doll! I mean a doll! A giant doll. He took photo after photo of one finger, one eye, a knee, a bit of her back—and I don't know what else! Can you imagine? For years and years he took photos of his wife, millimeter by millimeter. I think he's working on a tree now. Fantastic, don't you think? The life of a tree, in photos, from the moment it begins life till the time it is as big as a house."

After a short silence, he seems to remember they are waiting in the living room.

"And now what should I show these people to amuse them?"

He sifts through a stack of objects, leafs through some note-

The "King of Uranium," Joseph ▶
H. Hirshhorn, offers everything
he has, including his wife, Olga,
for a sculpture. He has already
given Picasso his jacket, and now
ties a bowtie around the neck of
the astonished artist.

Now Hirshhorn is in shirtsleeves, while Picasso sports his jacket and tie. This is the last time Steichen and Picasso will see each other.

Left: The Steichens and Hirshhorn (partially concealed by Douglas Cooper), Picasso, and the Justin K. Thannhausers. Right: Studying *Tête d'une Femme,* done in Vallauris in 1951.

books, and finally chooses the huge sheep's bell—I wonder why he has chosen the bell—and we return to the door that leads to the main room. Before opening it he stops, leaves the bell next to the window, and crosses his arms:

"And you don't know the man who came with Steichen?"

I fleetingly recall the little man who introduced himself as he came in but with whom I have had no time to exchange more than a few words. Without hesitation I put myself into the spirit of Picasso's nonsensical conversation game:

"What do you mean, not know him? He's the person who took your second show to New York."

"No, God no! He's the King of Uranium."

"He is?"

"Yes, sir. The King of Uranium. Why shouldn't there be a King of Uranium too? It seems he has mines everywhere, or something like that. Besides, he's a collector, from what I've been told, especially of sculpture."

These reflections suddenly make him decide not to show off the bell and he goes back to the living room to invite his guests down to the sculpture room.

Depending on the approach, the sculpture room is either on the ground floor or the basement of Notre Dame de Vie. Since the house is built on two ancient cultivation terraces, the sculpture studio can be entered from the lower terrace or from the main floor, which is built on the higher of the two terraces. Approaching the sculpture room through the long corridor on the main floor, a newcomer would assume it is in the basement. To his surprise, especially if the first visit to the house takes place in daylight, the "basement" boasts six huge windows that give onto the garden and admit the blazing light of the Mediterranean. There will be no surprise this time, however, since night

Left: Picasso turns *Tête d'une Femme* on its base for Steichen. Right: Hirshhorn, Picasso, Thannhauser, and Cooper—four great contemporary collectors.

has fallen and Jacqueline has asked me to go down before the visitors to turn on the lights. After I do that, I go to meet the guests. Hirshhorn and his wife are at the foot of the stairs, struck dumb by the spectacle in front of them. They have scarcely gone ten steps, but have already glimpsed some of Picasso's fabulous sculpture collection. It flashes across my mind that perhaps Hirshhorn is about to have a heart attack. From time to time he puts his hands to his head and murmurs something, not daring to go any farther:

"My God, have you seen that, Olga? My God!"

In a far corner Picasso and Steichen are talking. Steichen's young wife, who speaks decent French, occasionally acts the role of interpreter. I join them without their noticing, for they are absorbed in a lively conversation, and manage to take two quick photos before they become aware of my presence.

The photos I take later have to be managed with dizzying speed. With Picasso's characteristic ability not to miss a detail and to be involved in two or three things at once, he has noticed Hirshhorn at a distance, overwhelmed by the original bronze cast of a woman's head done in 1951.

"My God! My God!" Hirshhorn goes on exclaiming, as we approach. And turning toward me (I am suddenly transformed into an interpreter by force of circumstance), he says: "Tell Pablo I'll buy it."

I see by Picasso's expression the scant admiration this remark arouses. The answer could not be in any other language but Spanish. I realize it's only for my ears and best not translated for Hirshhorn:

"These collectors think of nothing but that: Buy, buy, buy!"

Fortunately, Hirshhorn saves the situation with a sudden humorous turnabout. He removes his jacket while continuing to talk, and politely insists that Picasso put it on.

25

"Tell him I'll give him everything I have for that sculpture, everything—my jacket, my tie, my money. Everything I own."

As he goes on talking, he takes off his bow tie, puts his hands in his pockets, and empties them of his wallet and a handful of papers and rumpled bills. He deposits everything in the hands of an astonished Picasso, who has been knotting Hirshhorn's tie. Picasso looks at me out of the corner of his eye.

"Ask him if he's going to give me his wife as well," he says, hardly able to suppress a smile.

"Of course. Everything I have," Hirshhorn answers, with a rapidity worthy of his host.

"The deal's closed," Picasso concludes, and everybody bursts into laughter.

While the merriment lasts, I move back a few yards to take some final photographs. Basically, I think, Hirshhorn has come out ahead. He has not managed to buy the sculpture, but he has won Picasso over.

Pablo moves away from the group around the sculpture for a moment and approaches me. It is obvious that he has still not recovered from the surprise of finding himself, for the first time in many a year, wearing a jacket and tie.

"What do you think of this costume?"

"Well, you look like a banker."

"A banker? That's right."

And then, turning quickly to his guests, he makes the gesture of a victorious *torero*. He raises the index finger of his right hand and shows it to the public in the plaza—in this case to famous collectors. That is how his friend Luis Miguel Dominguín gestured, for example, when he wanted to show he was unique in the bullfight.

"A banker? Yes, ladies and gentlemen. And now I would like to show you my collection."

In other words, with that gesture out of the explicit Andalusian bullfight language of his childhood he says: "You may all be very important collectors, but I am unique—I am the greatest collector of Picassos in the world."

After some lively conversation, we return to the first floor. The time for farewells has come. Picasso turns once more to his old friend of fifty years ago. He gazes at him with warmth, not knowing what to say. The silence seems endless, and I think I must be dreaming when I hear Picasso's last words to Steichen:

"Do you remember Gertrude Stein?"

Steichen does not seem to understand at first either, but finally he answers, after a long pause, full of nostalgia:

"Ah yes! Gertrude Stein . . . Gertrude Stein . . ."

"I am the greatest collector of ▶
Picassos in the world."

26

"To my surprise, a face takes shape on the page."

# CHAPTER 2

# An Afternoon at the Bullfight

7 August 1966

It is eleven on a Sunday morning. Picasso, wearing a dressing gown, is having a lively conversation with Douglas Cooper. The well-known critic is preparing *Picasso: Theatre,* a book he is readying for publication. Naturally, they are talking about the book's subject.

Picasso signs and inscribes a copy of the catalogue of a new ceramics exhibition for each of us. A moment later he remembers he has promised to give me a copy of the Italian edition of one of Hélène Parmelin's books and disappears to find it. He returns shortly and places the bulky volume on the table. On the first page he draws in the face of a bearded character, using three colors and bold strokes. I watch him from the other side of the table as he draws. To my surprise, a face takes shape on the page, as if Picasso were drawing upside down. The chin, the nose, the eyes of his creature are looking toward me, the hair toward him. He finishes the drawing and dedicates it without turning the page. I will realize later that there was a trick involved, but actually, from my vantage point, there is another head.

PICASSO: "That's true. I'll sign it from the other side, too, so it will be understood that it has to be looked at as if it were a playing card."

As he does that, he goes on: "All this about drawing is very mysterious. Often you're not aware you're drawing something else, seen in reverse or from one side or another. For instance, I remember something very peculiar that happened to me once, years ago, in a spiritualist session. Well, to be absolutely accurate, it was one of those salon spiritualist affairs. It's all the same, in any case. The medium made me do a drawing in the dark, so there could be no chance of a trick. My first attempt yielded nothing. It seems I couldn't throw myself into it wholeheartedly. In the last analysis, perhaps it was because I didn't really believe much in these things. Well, anyway, I tried hard not to think of anything, and, still in the dark, I did the drawing. You know, I remember it as if it had happened yesterday."

He then picks up a piece of paper and makes a complicated design without lifting his pencil. He shows the paper, turned obliquely, to all of us.

PICASSO: "What do you see?"

No one "sees" a thing. Picasso reverses the paper and we all see the face of a woman in profile, with regular features and a vaguely blurred mass of hair.

PICASSO: "Really fantastic, isn't it? Naturally the medium

The star of the afternoon.

identified her with the spirit of I don't know whom, someone out there. Anyone can think whatever he likes, but that doesn't make it any the less mysterious, does it?"

Today, for the first time, we are having lunch in the garden, under a pergola perched some fifty yards up the hill from the house. Picasso is wearing a brightly colored shirt and dark trousers. He has also put on a straw hat. This is an indication that he is in excellent form and that the period of convalescence has drawn to a close and become a chapter of recollections. Actually, for the last week he has gained strength steadily and given evidence of practically total recovery. All that is lacking, I think, is for him to feel the urge to go to the bullfight this afternoon. I say to Jacquèline: "If he goes to the bullfight today, tomorrow he'll begin to paint a canvas three yards long." Jacqueline smiles. Of course she would like Picasso to go to the bull-

Before the bullfight begins,
Picasso chats with Enrique Arias,
his friend, barber, and fellow
enthusiast.

fight, but at the same time she feels it may be a rash move, especially if he wears himself out to no purpose. "Anyway," she says, "Pablo is really quite well. If he feels up to it, we'll go to the bullfight. Why don't you suggest it at lunch?"

Six lobsters, a gift from Douglas Cooper, have been added to the usual luncheon fare. Picasso eats with the appetite of an adolescent and even drinks a few glasses of rosé. An easy, cheerful atmosphere prevails, and the warm sun, the wine, and the treat of the lobsters provide a propitious moment. We begin to talk about the bullfight scheduled for this afternoon.

PICASSO: "Are you going to the *corrida?* Do you have tickets? What if I'd like to go? No, no. First of all, I don't have a ticket. You mean there's one for me, too? And Jacqueline? And there's another one for Jacqueline, too? *Caramba,* you've thought of everything! Well, it's not that, no—it's because it's already too late—What are you saying? You think we'd make it if we left

Receiving gifts from the *picador.*

now? Well, I guess not. Besides, I have to dress. Of course, I could go this way. Maybe it would be all right if I just put on my wide-brimmed hat. Why don't I keep this one on? Well, because I'd rather wear another one."

Five minutes later we are speeding along the highway toward Fréjus. No sooner do we reach the city, where the half-ruined arches of the Roman aqueduct start, than we are forced to slow down to a snail's pace. Such is the crush of traffic, attracted by the last fight of the season. The superb amphitheater, which is frequently used as a bullring, is filled with spectators, mostly tourists. A human wave of unbelievable color floats upward to the top of the ancient arena, which was especially built for the Imperial soldiers at Julius Caesar's command. Two uniformed policemen act as our bodyguards through the lane next to the bullfighters' passage. Picasso seems overwhelmed by the tourists' outrageous hats, the miniskirts, the shorts, the shirts and blouses of every color in the rainbow. It is no longer the same as the fiesta of his childhood in Málaga, where all the shirts were white and the men seldom took off their jackets. Still, it is always the fiesta for him. Besides, for someone as sensitive as Picasso, the inevitable changes wrought by time on every aspect of life, including the spectacle of today's crowd, cannot be anything but stimulating.

At the arena with Cathy. When Picasso married Jacqueline, Cathy was four or five years old, and over the years Picasso has come to think of her as his own child.

The goring of a *torero*.

Right: After the "first bull," Picasso talks with Arias. Below: The Manila shawl included in the *picador*'s gifts is draped in front of Picasso's seat, clearly showing who is the most important spectator of the afternoon.

Another ear "for the best painter in the world."

"Fantastic," he says, as we walk together, arm in arm, looking to either side. "What do you think? Isn't it fantastic?"

I am not sure if he is referring to a group of "hippies," naked from the waist up, who watch our passage with an expression of several centuries of indifference, or to a couple of stoutish ladies in their fifties, attired in miniskirts, or simply to his presence today at the bullfight, together with painting the greatest passion of his life.

The two policemen have stationed themselves in the passageway just below Picasso, to keep the friendly but crushing siege of admirers at bay. It is no easy task. Tourists by the dozen approach, cameras at the ready, in quest of a photo-trophy of their vacation. A few manage to filter through the police guard, brandishing a paper or address book for the coveted autograph. The police react energetically, demonstrating their incorruptible professional zeal, and even the more importunate admirers finally desist. One little man, however, has inveigled his way through the barrier. He is Enrique Arias, a Spanish exile who is Picasso's personal friend and barber, the quintessential bullfight *aficionado* in the south of France. His commentary and observations are essential ingredients in Picasso's experience of the bullfight. He takes up his usual post four or five yards from his renowned compatriot, in the lane below or in the contiguous bullfighters' passage.

In the midst of a wild hubbub, as an enraged public shrieks at the bull for not rushing out, an old *picador* has recognized Picasso and clumsily rides toward him. He is grotesque in his huge boots and leather guard pads.

"It's *Fulano*," Arias says. (*Fulano* is not a surname as such, but when the surname is not known, *Fulano* is used. The English "what's-his-name" would be the closest equivalent.)

"*Fulano!*" Picasso exclaims.

And *Fulano* arrives, loaded with packages. A Manila shawl, exquisitely embroidered, is slung over his shoulder. The shawl is for "Don Pablo," and as he drapes it over the barrier in front of Picasso, everyone in the plaza realizes who is the most important spectator there. The packages contain Spanish specialties: brandy, sweets, red *chorizo* sausages, marzipan, almonds, all of which the *picador* has brought to France several times, beginning with the very first bullfight of the season, with the secret hope that Picasso may be present at one of them.

At last the first bull makes its entrance. It is a young bull, a *novillo*, small and nervous, and blind with rage. It charges against the wooden surrounds of the plaza and scratches its horns in the sand. It has not yet been worked by the cape when I hear Arias's powerful voice saying: "It's weak in the legs."

The bullfighter, Rafaelín Valencia, who is almost a child, barely has time to prove Arias's judgment. The young bull is on

Applauding the young *torero* who was gored.

its knees at the second pass of the cape. Picasso makes a slight gesture to show his admiration for Arias's knowledge of the bulls.

Rafaelín Valencia's second bull draws the same diagnosis from Arias, and the animal is on its knees several times, canceling out the excellent impression made by the bullfighter's series of superb full-circle passes to the right. The entire herd is weak, the *banderilleros* are gauche, the crowd heckles any and all moves by the *picadors,* unaware of the problems involved. It looks as if the *corrida* is off to a very bad start. Picasso and Arias are true *aficionados*. They refrain from voicing their judgments of the bullfighters.

The second *torero* of the afternoon is El Barquillero. He is flashier and more daring than Rafaelín, but he has no better luck with this herd of bulls. His first animal, also a *novillo*, has not been well worked by the *picador* and tosses the *torero* twice. Hysterical female cries can be heard. Picasso and Arias remain impassive.

Tossing back the *montera*, the bullfighter's hat; it is already in mid-air.

Before El Barquillero takes on his last bull, he dedicates it to Picasso:

"To the greatest painter in the world!" he shouts, throwing his hat up to the narrow lane in front of Picasso. Picasso catches it on the fly, thanks the *torero*, smiles, and salutes the bullfighter with his hand. However, he cannot help remarking, amused: "It's about time they figured out something else to say. Three bulls dedicated this afternoon, and all three "to the greatest painter in the world!"

El Barquillero, the red-draped sword or *muleta* in one hand, can scarcely manage a couple of decent passes. On the third pass he is spectacularly tossed. The animal turns in its tracks and repeatedly tramples the injured fighter. Everything has happened in a flash and the *peones*, El Barquillero's assistants, are too late to distract the bull and get it out of the *torero*'s path. The screaming crowd is beside itself. Several women faint. Picasso, on his feet for the first time during the fight, shakes his head from left to right. He is looking for Arias, who is discussing the unfortunate accident with Jacqueline. Meanwhile, El Barquillero has managed to get to his feet, with the help of his *peones*, but his knees are weak and he seems totally dazed. They take him by his arms to one side of the plaza.

The crowd, on the verge of hysteria, is shouting at the *torero* not to return to the arena. Without heeding this advice, well aware of his role, the young bullfighter limps to the middle of the ring and kills the bull with an imperfect thrust of the sword. Despite everything, the judges award him an ear for his courage and because of the crowd's insistence. El Barquillero ends his bullfighting afternoon with a turn around the ring worthy of Manolete.

Picasso and Arias are once again their impassive selves, two old *aficionados* indifferent to the agitation still stirring the plaza. They follow the work of the last bullfighter of the afternoon, Flores Elázquez. He fights the sixth bull beautifully, but kills it clumsily. This bull is also offered up to "the greatest painter in the world."

The strains of the last *pasodoble*, the unique music of the bull-fight, are still ringing in our ears when we leave the amphitheater under police protection. The police, who have remained at Picasso's side during the entire afternoon, manage with difficulty to keep the autograph hounds, the Sunday photographers, and the generally curious at bay. When the car comes, the youngest officer detains us a few minutes longer, as if to make sure that there is no danger of any more inopportune admirers following us. Only then do we realize that he has waited discreetly for any possible witness to be out of sight. With one hand he takes out a notebook, with the other he proffers a pen:

"Maître, if you please . . . "

Leaving the arena.

Unpacking and examining the documentation for the Chicago monument, *Woman from Chicago.*

# CHAPTER 3

# The Chicago Monument

Yesterday's bullfight is in the air at Notre Dame de Vie, as well as in Picasso's eyes and voice. It is impossible to talk of anything but bulls and bullfighters. Picasso is singing. He is singing songs about bulls, learned in childhood, that no one else any longer remembers:

> At Havana I stepped ashore
> while a violent, wild wind blew
> to search for Cáchares' sepulcher,
> one of the immortals few . . .

PICASSO: "Cáchares? Don't you know who Cáchares was? An immortal *torero*, just as the song says. Did I see him fight? Heavens no! He must have died, before I was born, in Havana. Listen, listen:

> And on the hard cold stone
> it was written there
> "Here lies Cáchares
> bullfighter without peer."

The last two lines are accompanied by an eloquent, almost *torero*-like gesture of the hand. Then, after a short pause, in a low and stately voice, he sings the end of the song:

> And all of us read it
> with emotion and respect
> as we thought of him then,
> and together we murmured:
> May God keep him and preserve him in heaven. Amen!

PICASSO: "The things that happen! How could I have seen Cáchares? People think I'm so old that one of these days they're going to ask if I ever saw Pepe Hillo fight. Just imagine! Though, come to think of it, I did see Lagartijo."

My knowledge of the bullfight leaves something to be desired. The proof is that I did not know Cáchares, but could place Lagartijo.

"Lagartijo? That can't be. Next you'll be telling me you've seen Frascuelo."

PICASSO: "Frascuelo no, but Lagartijo yes. I must have been ten years old when my father took me to see him fight. I remember his hair was white, snow white. In those days bullfighters didn't retire so young, as they do now. Well, the bulls were different then, too, huge—and they charged the horses as much as twenty times. And the horses dropped like flies, their guts everywhere. Horrible! Those days were different, and so was the bullfight."

Nostalgic, he recalls legendary names from the "art" of bullfighting. Guerrita, as great a *torero* as he was a *banderillero*. Today the experts consider him one of the pillars of the modern bullfight, though it may be for no other reason than that he retired a millionaire at 37. And Vicente Pastor, Bombita, Rafael El Gallo, Gallito, Gaona, most of them known to today's *aficionados* by hearsay and from having read about them a thousand times in the chronicles of the Fiesta of the Bull, without ever having seen them perform in the plaza. To have seen them, a spectator would have to be quite old—I make a mental calculation—and have begun to go to fights about 77 years ago, like Pablo Picasso.

PICASSO: "I also knew Cara Ancha, even if I never saw him fight. I was very young and my father, a great *aficionado*, took me to his hotel room in Málaga, either before or after the bullfight. I can't remember. It's one of my most vivid childhood recollections: I was on his lap looking up at him, overwhelmed."

The conversation is suddenly interrupted because a new character, weighed down with parcels, has entered the room. He is a tall, mature man, jovial and flushed with excitement. A

◀ Picasso studies the documentation for *Woman from Chicago* with William E. Hartmann, the architect, while Jacqueline looks on.

Picasso eats licorice drops to suppress his desire to smoke (he gave up cigarettes in 1965).

strange mixture of dynamic energy and soft shyness is his most striking characteristic. Since all the chairs in the living room are covered with objects, he deposits the packages he was clutching on the floor. Then he greets Picasso with a warm embrace, and the artist vanishes behind the athletic bulk of the latest arrival.

PICASSO: "How are you? It's a terribly long time since I've seen you."

While the man, moved by the encounter with Picasso, babbles some conventional French phrases, Picasso introduces us to Bill Hartmann, an architect from Chicago.

PICASSO, in Spanish: "You know, he's making a gigantic monument in Chicago based on one of my sculptures. It's similar to the Nesjar project in Marseilles, remember?"

He is referring to the Norwegian sculptor's visit a couple of months before. On that occasion we had the opportunity of seeing photos of the monument in progress.

PICASSO: "Now that I think it over, it occurs to me that the only two cities which have made public monuments out of my sculptures are Marseilles and Chicago. Do you think it has something to do with gangsters?"

Picasso points out a modification the architects found necessary.

Hartmann shows Picasso a photograph of the original sculpture and one of the maquette.

There is no time to translate the joke for the architect, who is completely occupied with one of his packages. He has already pulled out a metal tube containing the plans for the future sculpture and is handing them to Picasso, who is keen to see them immediately. He clears the only table in the living room to stretch them out.

Hartmann is speaking in English now, addressing himself to Jacqueline for her to translate. When Jacqueline leaves the room to bring drinks, I act as interpreter. As my English is fairly rudimentary, the dialogue eventually begins to take on the tone of a conversation among madmen. Picasso's impatience to grasp the tiniest details of the plans in the space of a split second does not help me in my task. The talk becomes confused and disjointed. Hartmann occasionally manages to answer directly in French.

As was to be expected, the plans encompass too many technical details for anyone with an imagination as overflowing as Picasso's. He quickly loses interest in deciphering the data. The conversation falls back on the simplest facts.

PICASSO: "How big is the monument?"

I am translating now from feet to meters:

"Fifty-three feet or 16 meters."

PICASSO: "What madness! Do you realize? Have you seen these plans? As I understand it, some twenty architects have

Jacqueline serves refreshments. Despite the telephone that never stops ringing, Jacqueline is keeping careful watch over Picasso's physical condition and following the discussion about the Chicago monument with great interest. Despite all these activities, she has found a moment to change her clothes.

been working on this for more than a year. If I thought of all that while I was working, I don't know if I'd be able to do it. Many times I do think of it, and it scares me."

While we are talking, Hartmann opens a cardboard box and takes a pile of photographic blow-ups from it. He spreads them out on the table. For Picasso, the photos are far more eloquent than the plans, and his interest is rekindled.

PICASSO: "Have you seen this? It's incredible!"

HARTMANN: "This is the original."

PICASSO: "Yes, yes, I see."

HARTMANN: "And this is our model. Later, I'll show you some modifications which were necessary for technical reasons."

Picasso devours photograph after photograph with his eyes. One of them is taken from an angle which clearly shows one of the modifications. Hartmann explains:

"The sheets of metal that you see here are slightly thicker than

Picasso studies photomontages showing two possible sites for the monument.

the original, for greater resistance. Among other things, the wind that comes up from the lake in Chicago can often be quite violent. For the same reason we have also added a support here to reinforce it."

Picasso looks at the last photograph with curiosity. He seems pleased at the results. However, he has still not disclosed whether or not he approves of the work done by the architects.

HARTMANN, quite aware of this: "Tell him it is really a very small change." And to make it clear, he turns to Picasso and says: "Petit. Très petit."

While he carries on in a passionate tone of voice, his large, clear eyes are fixed intently on Picasso's gaze. I realize the man from Chicago is playing for the highest stakes, for all he is worth. If Picasso should decide not to accept a single modification—something that is quite possible—Hartmann and his team will have worked for over a year in vain. However, Picasso seems totally unaware of the architect's anxiety and his decision is postponed until the following day, so that he can study the two series of photographs carefully.

A sequence of photomontages which show possible settings for the monument is now spread out on the table.

HARTMANN: "Another problem is this—the place for the monument. Here is the spot we originally had in mind. How-

48

Impatient as a child, Picasso
attacks a package of gifts
Hartmann (with his back to the
camera) has brought. The poet
Rafaël Alberti's daughter, Aitana,
looks on.

ever, a fountain was there and everybody thought it so lovely . . . ''

To my surprise, I am suddenly translating with comparative
ease. Picasso sits down and is absolutely silent. He moves his
head rhythmically.

HARTMANN: "Now we think this other spot would be better,
behind the courthouse."

Picasso looks at both photos and says that, yes, it would be
better. Hartmann is unable to conceal his delight. There is no
definite answer yet, but it is almost an answer.

There is a short interlude for refreshments. Someone calls on
the telephone from Paris and Picasso disappears into his bedroom for a moment. He will take advantage of the occasion to

change his showy robe for a colorful shirt, no less garish even though darker-toned. The American now begins to look around for something he seems to have lost among the chair legs. It is a second cardboard box. He finally locates it among the disorder of objects strewn around the floor.

"*J'avais oublié*—I had forgotten—the *cadeaux*" he explains, in an awkward predicament between English and French.

Picasso lunges for the box with all the impetus of his proverbial child's curiosity. His eyes are giving off sparks and his hands are trembling slightly as he unties the knots in the string. He barely manages to pull off the top when he is shouting enthusiastically:

"A straw hat! A straw hat!"

Hat on head, he pulls another package out of the box. A striped apron appears. He puts it on in a flash. Hartmann explains that the outfit—hat and apron—is worn by fish dealers somewhere in America. Picasso, repressing his natural gaiety, says quickly, in all seriousness:

"It's very good, very good. And it's also very useful in working with ceramics."

He disappears into his studio and returns quickly, wearing not the new striped apron but an old leather one. He proudly shows off his favorite outfit for working with ceramics or sculpture and gives a practical demonstration of how he can clean his hands on it. Everybody realizes that he is showing his appreciation of Hartmann's gifts in his own highly original manner. Because—even though no one knows it—Picasso is enormously shy.

Not knowing what to do or say after pondering the merits of his leather apron, Picasso goes back to talking about the sculpture and asks about the model they have built in Chicago. The architect seems to have been waiting for this question. He answers in a rather mysterious tone, this time in impeccable French:

"Perhaps tomorrow. I think it will arrive tomorrow."

9 August 1966

Five-thirty in the afternoon. From the first floor terrace I see a small truck pull up. Two men slowly unload a wooden box while Hartmann looks on nervously. At the foot of the stairs that lead to the sculpture room I meet Picasso, who says jokingly:

"These Americans really are quick! Yesterday they order the model from Chicago and today it's in the house."

When we go into the studio, the two men have already set up the model on a movable easel six or seven yards from the original. Picasso proudly struts back and forth across the enormous room. He stops, crosses his arms, and inspects each sculpture alternately. The architect trails after him, searching

"A straw hat! A straw hat!"

Picasso's expression for some reassuring sign. For the hundredth time they go up to the model and turn it on the stand. Suddenly, as if he had made an irrevocable decision, and laughing heartily, Picasso walks over to where I am standing, beside the famous sculpture of a pregnant woman:

"I think it's really fantastic, don't you? In fact, I'd go so far as to say it's better than the original."

When Hartmann realizes that Picasso has given his approval, he cannot conceal his joy, a joy which explodes his usual shyness into a thousand pieces.

Half an hour later, as I help him replace the model in its box, Bill Hartmann, bubbling over in unexpected loquacity, confides in me:

"He's marvelous," he says, talking about Picasso. "Charming, incredible, and unique."

I remark on the series of ups and downs Hartmann has had to live through during the last twenty-four hours. He says:

"Just imagine. Pablo could have turned it down as easily as not, and instead . . . "

"And instead," I answer, "not only has he said yes, but he

Picasso and Hartmann pose with the maquette, which has just arrived from Chicago.

has also refused to take the check you brought in the name of the city of Chicago. All in all, a very good day for you, Bill, don't you agree?"

"Oh, yes! Good. In fact, marvelous. An excellent day, really!"

We are referring to something that happened a few minutes before:

Immediately after Picasso's "yes," we return to the first-floor living room. Hartmann stops smiling for a moment, takes a paper out of his briefcase, and places it on the table. Everything goes so quickly that I do not see the amount written on the check.

HARTMANN: "And now we are going to talk about money."

Picasso scarcely looks at the paper. Nor does he realize it is a check. He turns it over and pushes it to the other end of the table. His reaction, in Spanish, is practically a lament:

"*Caramba!* Isn't there any way for these Americans to take a gift? How do you say it in English? Go on, tell him!"

And suddenly turning to Hartmann, without giving me time to utter a word, he says alternately in French and in Spanish:

"It's a gift, for heaven's sake, a gift."

53

Picasso and Hartmann examine the maquette and compare it with the original sculpture.

Hartmann, overwhelmed, protests and scarcely knows what to do. Then Picasso makes everything perfect in his incomparable way:

"Look, it's more *charming* this way."

The architect realizes that Picasso has made use of perhaps the only word he knows in English and finally surrenders, a bit taken aback amidst the general hilarity, "charming" hilarity, the most "charming" of the day.

Mr. Hartmann's extraordinary day is far from over, however. He remembers that he promised to telephone Chicago to relay the outcome of his mission. Picasso, amused, will not let him leave:

"Come, come, you'll have time enough to telephone the mayor tomorrow. Stay with us now."

Torn between his pleasure at being with Picasso and his desire to communicate the happy news to his colleagues, Hartmann begins to wring his hands. Suddenly he remembers something else and leaps out of his chair:

"The original! Ask Pablo what we should do with the original in Chicago. Tell him that if he likes, we can send it back immediately."

He is referring to the second original of the sculpture. As is his custom, Picasso has had two copies of *Woman from Chicago* cast in bronze. He keeps one in his studio and had sent the other to Hartmann to use as a basis for the Chicago model.

PICASSO: "The original? Good heavens, what would I want the original for now? I'd have a thousand problems with the customs authorities. Ask him if they have a museum or some other place in Chicago where they can store it."

Hartmann cannot believe his ears.

"*Merci*, Pablo," he manages between gasps. "Thank you, thank you—it is really too much—too much for me and for Chicago . . . "

The conversation is almost entirely in Spanish now, for we are carrying on from where we left off with the bullfighters Frascuelo, Bombita, Cara Ancha, and Gaona. The great names from the past have again captured Picasso's fancy. Naturally, with all this going on, it is impossible for Hartmann to join in the conversation. Fortunately, he knows how to listen attentively even when he cannot understand. In a few moments the subject changes to Picasso's well-known piece for theater, *Desire Caught by the Tail*, of which the author is smilingly proud.

"They've even put it on in Japan," he says as he disappears behind a door, only to reappear a moment later with a manuscript in hand.

"You mean you don't know this play? I didn't write it very long ago. Of course, how could you? It hasn't been published!" And, sitting down on a white chair, he puts on his glasses and begins reading *The Burial of Count Orgaz*, an unpublished play in poetry—to give it some sort of classification—about twenty typed pages long. After reading the title, he feels some clarification is in order. Giving Hartmann a cursory glance over the tops of his glasses, he says:

"The characters have no names, just numbers." Then, after a few words explaining the situation, he continues reading:

    1: There's nothing but oil and old clothes here.
    2: Son of a bitch, whore, cuckold, double cuckold, with rheumatism of a wolf and a limping owl.
    0: Child of winking flowers and gossip, perched above the greasepaint pot, child of twisted nail rent open with the point of a knife.

2: The little Rat Pérez dressed up as a priestling spraying the leathery clothes of the dark.

1: Having received an open envelope and stamp, the postman or his grandmother can eat it without having to explain anything to any happy creature.

2: But what has to be done is to untie and tie up the ball of string and pluck the wind from the candle.

1: Cold- and hot-bloodedly break down doors and windows and start throwing gloves and lions and partridges.

0: High-hatted gossamer.

2: Two thieves.

1: And the wailing of the whooping-up.

The reading continues for a good half hour, only interrupted from time to time by one of Picasso's marginal comments. I occasionally burst into wild laughter. Picasso writes in the same way he talks about the two villages he invented. Spanish villages and Spanish situations, very familiar to me since I have heard him improvise on these themes dozens of times. It all smacks of childhood, Málaga, a southern Andalusian family, a picaresque novel, the bits and pieces of village life, everything told in his special Spanish, Picassoid, but universal sense of humor.

"And here we come to the end of our story, as well as of the banquet. Not even the madman knows how it all turned out. The postman's wife went to the bullfight with her cousin. The postman fled with the sister of his sister-in-law Amalia. His nephew didn't know what he did all afternoon or what time he finally made it home. He didn't go home that night or the next day either. Then he made a scene. But on his Aunt Regueldo's saint's day, in the middle of the banquet, the meringue exploded. Perdaguino's daughter made a fart, pulled her tits out of her blouse, lifted her skirt, and showed her pussy. Just imagine the priest's face, and the little nephew's voice, and the goatherd's girls, and the little whores from in front, and the nuns crossing themselves, and everyone dying of laughter from so much lightning and thunder."

"Tra lala lala la——

"Toreador toreador toreador."

Picasso begins to laugh so heartily that he has to stop reading several times to wipe the tears from his cheeks. During one of these breaks, I turn to Bill Hartmann, who is sunk in a discreet and admiring silence a thousand leagues from the fabulous text for which we are playing the part of audience.

"What a pity you don't understand Spanish."

"Oh, no, it's nothing—it's like listening to Mozart."

Picasso shows his appreciation of the compliment with a big smile and continues reading, unperturbed:

"In bed, Las Meniñas play at burying the Count Orgaz . . . "

"It's a gift, for heaven's sake, a gift."

# CHAPTER 4

# Twenty Years of Ceramics

Picasso's white Lincoln winds along the half-deserted route that goes from Mougins to Vallauris. The August dog days are upon us. The sun at four-thirty in the afternoon beats down, hot and muggy. Fortunately, a pleasant breeze comes through the car windows. Picasso is singing:

> At Havana I stepped ashore
> while a violent, wild wind blew
> to search for Cáchares' sepulcher
> one of the immortals few.

Without a stop he then goes on to sing endless songs from the *zarzuela*, the Spanish equivalent of light opera. He sings some very well-known ones and others totally forgotten, humming the lines when he does not remember the words. Finally he sings a popular Spanish song he says he has just learned and knows perfectly:

> Olive picker there
> harvest your trees,
> Would you give me three small olives
> so my little boy can play?

After a long silence, when we are all convinced he has forgotten the rest of the song, he starts again, as naturally as a professional singer:

> The virgin is walking
> across the dark mountain.
> At the flight of a partridge
> the mule takes fright.

Turning a bend in the road, we come into Vallauris. The first building on the road from Mougins is a half-finished apartment house. We can scarcely refrain from commenting on the urban transformation of Vallauris during the last few years.

PICASSO: "Vallauris really is ugly, isn't it? I don't know. A few years ago it wasn't so awful. It was never a marvel by any means, but it had a certain charm. The ceramics factories are all hidden by new buildings now. Some are abandoned. Just the same, modern buildings are not as hideous as people think. I like them."

It seems the Maestro is becoming more and more optimistic. Or perhaps it is because he feels more Spanish than ever today, and so is in a mood to be perverse. The truth is that the Vallauris of 1966 is a far cry from those magical landscapes he himself painted between 1949 and 1951. Those paintings are full

◄ At the opening of the Galería Madoura exhibition, before the arrival of the general public. Picasso created all his ceramic works in the studio adjoining the gallery, from 1946 to 1966.

At the Galería Madoura with
Jacqueline and a young friend
who enjoys going on outings with
the Picassos.

Top: With the gallery's director, Suzanne Ramier. Center: Checking a frame. Bottom: Picasso and Jacqueline chat with George and Suzanne Ramier.

On the opening day of the exhibition, Picasso created his last three "real" ceramic works. The first of them, shown in these pages, was the best.

of russet and wine-red chimneys and rooftops set against a pale-blue sky or the golden green of surrounding hills. Even his winter landscapes of that period are "happier" than this summer wasteland of poorly constructed, monolithic building blocks, crowded together in a massive urban disorder and totally lacking in style.

The automobile crosses the Place de la Liberation. To the right is a cast of *L'Homme au Mouton*, and to the left the chapel named *La Guerre et la Paix*. The town hall where Picasso married Jacqueline Roque one June day in 1960 is nearby. Jacqueline has told me of her surprise and emotion when Picasso ordered the car to stop in front of the town hall, and said: "I bet you can't guess what we're going to do here. We're going to get married."

A little farther on is the Place de L'Ecole, where a bullfight in Picasso's honor recently took place. Two well-known bull-fighters killed a pair of bulls each, even though killing the bull is strictly prohibited in Vallauris. Behind *L'Homme au Mouton* is the Rue de Fournas, where Picasso kept a studio for several years and painted "miles and miles of canvases," to use his expression. Naturally he sees Vallauris in a special way, despite the modern buildings. Vallauris represents, in a certain sense, Picasso's own last twenty years.

The automobile now moves slowly through the Avenue

Clemenceau. As a result of the "Picasso boom," the street is lined with dozens of ceramics shops, their wares displayed in showcases along the narrow sidewalks. Thousands of tourists come through this street every year, attracted by the publicity myth of "Vallauris-Picasso." Eventually they buy some grotesque ashtray which has nothing at all to do with the Spanish artist and his mastery of traditional craftsmanship.

"What else can they do?" he remarks pityingly. "Basically, they're not to blame if people like ugly things."

As in the case of the apartment blocks, it is useless to argue. Nor is he saying what he really thinks.

We get out of the car at the back patio of the Galería Madoura. It is situated in an eighteenth-century building that has been superbly restored. There are still two hours or so before the exhibition, "20 Years of Picasso Ceramics," is to begin, but the author of it all wants to see it before the public and honored guests arrive. We quickly cross the studio where Picasso worked from 1946 until his recent surgery. During a lightning visit a few days ago I saw him paint his first three ceramics in less than fifteen minutes—after an imposed absence of almost a year. Although I do not know it at the moment, these three ceramics are to be Picasso's very last. During his final years he will devote himself exclusively to engraving, drawing, and painting. As we watched him work, his concentration and pleasure thinly disguised behind a little smile, I recalled one of Sabartès's anecdotes.

Picasso's lifelong friend wrote of the artist's amazement in 1946 at the technical vocabulary he was learning in this very studio— "flamme libre . . . email cuit . . . couvettes sur silicate . . . sulfuro . . . caissons soufflés . . . fondants . . . englobes . . . plein feu"—and so many other words, all new and full of magical-poetical overtones.

Picasso guesses at our hurry to see the ceramics in the hall above the studio, and deliberately keeps us at the foot of the stairs.

"One minute, ladies and gentlemen. We are in the Patio de Caballos, and there are still five minutes before the bull-fight——"

And it truly *is* a bullfight, a most fantastic one: 120 original pieces, almost all of them unknown and almost all the property of the artist. Round, oval, square plates, tiles, glasses, vases, in classical shapes and whimsical shapes, heads of bulls, pink owls and white owls, erotic motifs, period scenes from the second half of the nineteenth century, suns, fried eggs, fruit, men with long hair and with short hair, dancers, centaurs, fauns, bullfighters, *picadors*, painters, sculptors, landscapes, fish, bouquets of flowers, pigeons, musicians, monkeys, condors, bullrings filled with spectators or eerily empty, Jacqueline here, Jacqueline there, Jacqueline in every color under the sun. The ceramics alone, without reference to the painting, sculpture, drawing, and engraving, strike one not as the output of a single man but of an entire civilization. On some future day, we think, dazzled,

Applying the finishing touches.

someone will discover the Picasso Civilization, as if it were the Maya Civilization, or the Aztec Civilization. The ceramics alone would suffice to give the impression of an entire civilization.

Picasso wanders back and forth, from one ceramic to another, glowing with satisfaction. He is an Andalusian, as the whole world knows, and like any good Andalusian he has only two possible moods: melancholy and joy. Today he woke up melancholy, but now there is not a happier soul in the universe.

Radiating charm, he jokes with and signs catalogues for friends and for those he has worked with in the gallery. Then he chats enthusiastically with the gallery owners, Suzanne and Georges Ramier, who taught him the rudiments of the potter's trade twenty years ago. Surely they did not suspect then the trouble their pupil would cause them by inventing new combinations and techniques, modeling works that would eventually revolutionize traditional ceramic style. And perhaps his new style will put an end to any further invention, just as one day in 1907, with the *Demoiselles d'Avignon*, he put an end to a certain kind of painting. But meanwhile, the craftsmen on the Avenue Clemenceau, only twenty yards away, go on making the most hideous ceramics in the world.

"Picasso seems to have been transformed into three leprechauns dashing about the room at once, such is the speed with which he plays hide-and-seek with the paintings."

# CHAPTER 5

# In the "Secret Room"

We are gathered in the living room at Notre Dame de Vie. The merry sound of the bells that hang at the door momentarily interrupts the lively conversation. The Spanish maid comes in and tells us that a man with a name she cannot pronounce is at the garden gate.

"Rosh Horn," she says, "or Rosch Hirn, or something like that."

"Rothschild?" Picasso asks.

"I really didn't catch it. Maybe it's that. At least it sounded like that."

"Well, tell him I'm not here. That I've gone out or that I'm at the dentist. Tell him what you like."

Picasso has nothing against his old friend, Baron Philippe de Rothschild, whom he would certainly welcome under other circumstances. The incident does not surprise any of us, however, for we all know that Picasso hates being interrupted when he is working or entertaining. This has managed to irritate most of his friends at one time or another, for they have all experienced what Baron de Rothschild is experiencing today. That is, if it *is* the Baron and not Joseph Hirshhorn, who has an invitation.

PICASSO: "What? Maybe it's Hirshhorn and not Rothschild? Perhaps you're right. I don't really remember what day I told him to come. Why don't you go and look? If it's Rothschild, act the idiot, as if you were just walking around, and go on walking as naturally as possible. You don't know him anyway, do you? So, in that case, it will be easy to act the idiot. If it's Hirshhorn, on the other hand, open the gate and let him in."

There is no cynicism in Picasso's words, but rather a note of mischief. Besides, it would be foolish to think he preferred Hirshhorn, whom he has only seen once, to the Baron. But Picasso is a man of his word, and has made a formal commitment to Hirshhorn, while Rothschild would simply be an unexpected arrival, to be treated like any other. In fact, only recently I heard Picasso speak of the Baron with a mixture of affection and surprise, as he opened a bottle of "Mouton Rothschild" at dinner:

"Can you imagine, he wanted me to draw a *mouton*—a sheep, in other words—with a bunch of grapes hanging from its mouth. I suppose he wanted to use it on a label for his wine or to decorate his castle in Bordeaux. Besides, he wanted a sculpture from me. Absolutely mad! He'll probably have to wait like those millionaire Argentinians in Paris. Thirty years ago they asked me to paint a door. I never painted it and never will. There

One of the many *Baigneuses* of the 1920s.

Sorting out works from ▶
various periods.

are painters who accept orders and others who don't. I don't. Besides, times have changed since the French Revolution. Or haven't they?"

I follow Picasso's instructions carefully and stroll along the hundred yards or so that separate the house from the garden entrance. Before reaching the gate, the road curves slightly to bypass a hundred-year-old water oak. From here I recognize Hirshhorn's silhouette on the other side of the gate. His wife is with him. He greets me effusively, for he has recognized me, too, and knows now that he has not waited in vain.

Hirshhorn's good humor increases as we enter the house and move toward the living room. His high spirits are perfectly understandable when one thinks what it must mean to a collector of modern art to visit Picasso. Besides, Hirshhorn is not only a great collector, but also a "self-made man," American style, and absolutely indifferent to the prejudices of his European counterparts. Thus, he is not at all embarrassed to show his delight openly, and now he begins to dance a solo fox-trot while singing "I Can't Give You Anything But Love, Baby." The spectacle amuses Picasso enormously. Without taking his eyes from Hirshhorn, who is now singing a rhythmic cha-cha-cha

from the other side of the table in the living room, he starts talking in Spanish:

"Just look at this nut! Did I tell you he's offered to lend some of my sculptures from his collection for that show in Paris? It turns out he has one of my earliest pieces, something I did years and years ago. He's really nice, isn't he?"

Jacqueline has already spoken to me about the homage exhibition, but she also told me that Picasso has more or less refused. His commentary on Hirshhorn's generosity makes me think he might be changing his mind, despite his dislike of homage exhibitions.

No matter. Whether or not there will be an exhibition in Paris, Picasso has decided to reciprocate Hirshhorn's generous gesture. He invites us to go next door to the studio. No sooner is he aware of Olga Hirshhorn's admiration of a superb ceramic —a woman's face drawn on a bit of roof tile—than he presents it to her as a gift, with his dedication. The King and Queen of Uranium are, of course, deeply affected, and their show of emotion befits the circumstances.

But Picasso the magician and consummate charmer has not shown all his cards. He knows Hirshhorn is a great collector and he knows what it takes to dazzle and impress one. He takes us

An African sculpture broods over the busy scene.

to the mysterious room where he hides his most valued treasures.

The "secret room"—at least that is what we call it in our invented language at Notre Dame de Vie—is worthy of its name. First of all, because it is always locked, and Picasso keeps the key in one of his pockets. It is the only key he carries. Secondly, because he not only stores the oldest "Picassos" there—and those he most treasures—but because the better part of the paintings in his private collection are also there. Cézannes, Renoirs, Degases, Derains, Bonnards, Corots, Douanier Rousseaus are stacked helter-skelter along with Modiglianis, Matisses, Mirós, Braques, and a Juan Gris. The smaller canvases are piled one atop the other; the larger ones are turned facing the wall. (This is the collection which Jacqueline will give to the Louvre after Picasso's death, apparently carrying out a wish he expressed during his lifetime.)

Penetrating the dense gloom is akin to visiting a half-abandoned attic, where odds and ends are stored. Only a recent Picasso painting, on the wall opposite the door, can be distinguished. It seems to be hanging there to put the initiate off the track, for it is a painting from the 1950s, on one of his familiar themes—that of the painter and the model. The paintings in the secret room are not always the same, however.

Cézanne's *L'Estaque* is propped against the wall. On the chest is a portrait of Jaime Sabartès.

They are accustomed to "traveling" about the house. One of Picasso's favorite entertainments consists in taking canvases from one place to another to look at them in different lights. Perhaps this explains the presence of the interloper.

Jacqueline draws the curtains, and the room expands before our eyes. There is a feeling of spaciousness, an impression of relatively few canvases. But how many are stored there? Five hundred? A thousand? Or millions and millions, as the exaggerating, Andalusian Picasso would have it?

No sooner do we enter the room than a "bullfight" begins. Picasso picks up a large canvas and turns it to show his improvised audience of *aficionados*. *Olé!* It's a Cézanne. Another canvas, and *Olé!*—another Cézanne!

While Picasso moves back to contemplate and discuss the paintings, I sense Hirshhorn behind me, enthralled. Not only has he seen two Cézannes, but also a Modigliani head in a corner of the room and a few small canvases that face outward. These last are three paintings from the Blue Period, and a minuscule portrait of Picasso's sister painted when he was an adolescent. There is no doubt that Hirshhorn has just realized where he has been brought.

Picasso seems to have been transformed into three or four

leprechauns dashing about the room at once, such is the speed with which he plays hide-and-seek with the paintings.

Someone says:

"Slower, for goodness sake. This is awful!"

The spectacle is truly hallucinatory. Picasso continues his maniacal task as if he wanted to show his entire treasure trove at once, as if he had counted out the minutes in which to do it. Suddenly, between one canvas and another, he bumps into me:

"You were asking about Juan Gris the other day? Look here, I only have this one. That's life! I would like to have others, of course, but the opportunity slipped by. He died so young."

He is referring to his practice of exchanging paintings with other contemporaries, especially with Braque and Matisse. I want to answer him, but he is already talking with someone else about the two Cézannes or about the Le Nain at the right of one of them. But he has not forgotten Hirshhorn, who

To the left of Cézanne's *L'Estaque* is his *Le Château Noir*. Both have been given to the Louvre, in accordance with Picasso's wishes.

A Modigliani portrait peeps out of a corner.

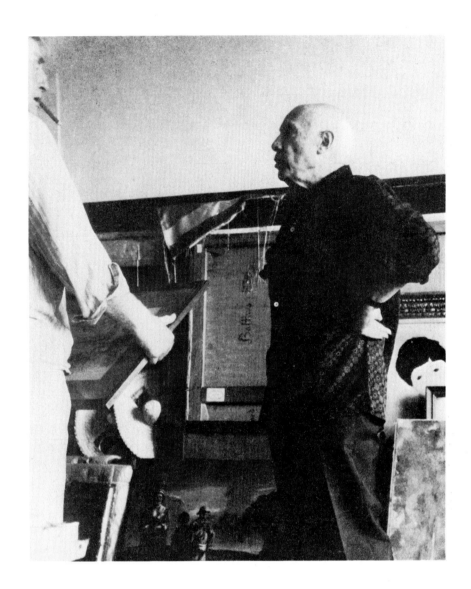

remains in his corner, dumbfounded, looking at everything open-mouthed.

"Do I have a Rousseau? Of course."

And he brings out, almost simultaneously, two huge Rousseaus whose fantastical figures are almost life-size.

Pablo Picasso the collector is satisfied with the effect on his American colleague. Yet he wants to add a final fillip by making a declaration worthy of the role he is acting out:

"Tell him I bought these two Rousseaus for five pesetas each."

When I start to translate, Picasso stops me and raises his right index finger emphatically at Hirshhorn while he shouts in the pidgin of the street vendor:

"One dollard——one dollard chaqu'un——"

As Picasso helps Jacqueline, he alternates between grumbling
and joking. Above: Maurice Jardot, art critic and director of the
Galerie Louise Leiris in Paris, lends a hand.

# CHAPTER 6

# Jacqueline's Homage

André Malraux, one of Picasso's old friends and Minister of Culture in General de Gaulle's cabinet, has sent a representative to propose an official exhibition in homage of the artist. The idea is to mount a show of proportions heretofore unheard of for the work of any living painter. Picasso rejects the idea totally and tells his friends:

"Just what I needed, an homage show. As if I ever accepted an homage in my life! What's more, the very idea of it has always seemed idiotic to me. Even as a boy, I remember, I was once supposed to receive a medal in Málaga. I never even went to the place where it was being given."

But a chance circumstance will make the exhibition a reality. Picasso is still convalescing from his operation and the doctors insist he take some mysterious pills. They are meant to keep him from painting, although he does not know this. They are to make him sleep. When he wakes from his siesta, a Spanish custom he has never before observed, he is on edge—nervous and occasionally bad-tempered. Jacqueline decides to invent a variety of games to distract him, to make him forget that, also for the first time in his life, he has stopped painting. Among the games Jacqueline invents is the game of discreetly convincing him to accept Malraux's invitation. A second representative of Malraux's is sent to visit—the critic Jean Leymarie, who works in Switzerland, arrives at Notre Dame de Vie. He and Picasso are on very good terms. Thus, the homage exhibition becomes a reality, thanks to Jacqueline's decision and despite the painter's initial reluctance.

3 October 1966

We are in the "secret room" again. Jean Leymarie has left for Paris a few days ago and has forgotten a fundamental detail: to measure the paintings which will go on exhibition at the Grand Palais in six weeks. There is a constant coming and going. Jacqueline, Louise Leiris, and the director of the gallery, Maurice Jardot, are in the process of correcting Leymarie's oversight, recognizing that he was the victim of a tremendous emotional experience.

"*Femme Assise*, 1963," Jacqueline shouts from behind a painting turned upside down. And, after a brief pause, the measurements in millimeters: "130 by 195."

Maurice Jardot takes notes in a corner, steadily but without hurry, his notebook resting on the upper edge of a Modigliani. Jacqueline continues: "*Femme Nue Renversée* . . . 130 by 170 . . . April, 1932 . . . *Homme à la Mandoline*, 158 by 71 . . . 1911

. . . *Nature Morte Espagnole,* 46 by 33 . . . 1912." Occasionally, she only makes reference to the professional enumeration of the painting: "*L'Atelier de Cannes* . . . that's an 80." Or: "Another 100 . . . *Acrobate* . . . 1930."

While I help her turn an enormous painting that was facing a wall, Jacqueline remarks: "I don't know how Leymarie is going to do a catalogue without the measurements. What if we played a joke on him and sent not only the forgotten measurements but added more paintings than he expects? He'll have more work with the catalogue, but he'll enjoy it more. Don't you think so?"

And then she calls out in a high voice: "*La Cuisine* . . . 1948 . . . 175 by 250."

In a flash we are all Jacqueline's accomplices, except for Picasso, who is just coming through the door. To his amazement we are adding a canvas similar to *Femme Nue Renversée,* which had already been chosen with his consent, to those going to Paris.

PICASSO: "Not that one. Let's see." Then, turning to me, he says: "Can't you see you've already included one just like it?"

JACQUELINE, with a look of descending from the clouds: "Oh. All right. But it's very beautiful."

PICASSO: "If it's like that, go ahead. You can put in anything you like. I don't give a damn."

By suppertime more than ten canvases have been added to Leymarie's list.

JACQUELINE: "*Femme Nue sur la Plage,* 1937."

PICASSO: "How many women on the beach do you expect to send! What will they think of me in Paris? They'll say I never paint anything but naked women on the beach."

JACQUELINE: "Oh, no, Pablo, they won't say anything. They'll see that each one is different."

4 October 1966

Eight o'clock at night. We are still playing yesterday's game in the "secret room," adding paintings to the already long list which Leymarie chose for the exhibition. Jacqueline thinks that instead of the sixty or seventy they expect in Paris, "we'll surprise them and send at least ninety or a hundred."

Picasso, who at first joined the game unwittingly, is now personally selecting some of the added canvases. According to Jacqueline, who knows him so well, he seems to have understood the nature of the game instinctively and the roles have now been reversed.

PICASSO: "Let's see—where's the *Hommage à Manet?*"

The canvas is found behind a stack piled in a corner of the "secret room." We carry it to the middle of the room with Jardot's help. Picasso backs away a few steps and looks at it for

Applying fixative to *Hommage à Manet.* This painting, done in Paris in 1919, is better known by its original title, *Les Amoureux.* It measures 73 × 55 inches. ▶

a long time, his arms crossed over his chest in a familiar gesture. But this time there is a trace of humor in his pose. I have seen him make this gesture on other occasions, imitating an imaginary painter contemplating an imaginary canvas.

PICASSO: "*Caramba!* The little cat has been erased. I'll draw it in again with charcoal. Besides, it has to have fixative and the word 'Manet' has to be written in at the top. What do you think? Malraux wants to give me an homage show? Well, I want to do the same for Manet! To each his own."

Picasso and I are alone while the others go to the living room for an aperitif. We are talking about Spain, as usual, but especially about the imaginary villages we invented in a conversation long ago. An eavesdropper would think we were totally mad if he chanced to listen in on one of our Surrealistic chats. Fortunately, we seldom talk this way in front of other people.

PICASSO: "And tell me, my dear Don Enrique, since you've

Picasso touches up the charcoal drawing of a cat on *Hommage à Manet*, which has become faint with the passage of time. His hand is as steady as that of a young man.

just come from Navas de Malvivir . . . excuse this aside, but the snow and the condition of the roads . . . you're really brave!"

I: "That's how it is, Don Hilario, though I'm a bit ashamed to tell you. Can you imagine, ten horses gave out from the time we left the village."

The game consists not only of inventing outlandish talk about a fictitious Spanish village, but also of talking ceremoniously, sententiously, like characters in a certain kind of turn-of-the-century novel. Picasso has dubbed me Don Enrique Salgado, and I have given him the name Don Hilario Cuernajón Núñez de Vaca, a name which particularly delights him.

PICASSO: "Well, as I was saying, you just arrived. Tell me what's new in Navas de Malvivir?"

I: "It hasn't moved an inch, Don Hilario. It's still in just the same place. And if it weren't for the troubles we've been having with the neighboring village, Ataquines de Todos los Rodiezmos, it wouldn't be worth talking about."

PICASSO: "I know, I know. I read the newspapers. That priest is furious because they want to steal the statue of the Macarena and take it to their village. You see, everybody knows everything. There's no news that doesn't get around, nor evil that doesn't last a hundred years, nor good from which some evil doesn't come, nor painter who doesn't eventually get himself an homage show. What barbarians these Spaniards are! Who would ever think of that? Steal the Macarena from the priest at Navas de Malvivir! And he ill besides."

1: "But, as you probably suspected, Don Hilario, that business about his being sick is not all . . . "

PICASSO: "Do you think I don't know the whole story? Do you think I'm living in an ivory tower, or in the fifteenth century, or that I'm just a country bumpkin? Go on! I subscribe to the ABC [the monarchist newspaper published in Madrid], and there's no news that's not in the ABC. You're talking about the postman's daughter, I mean the priest's, and as everyone knows they're all just a pack of whores."

1: "I don't mean to offend you, Don Hilario, they're your cousins as well, and all of us know . . . "

PICASSO: "What's all this rubbish about offending me? The truth is the truth and we'd better call bread bread and wine wine and a spade a spade. And as they say in Spain: 'White on black or white on white, it's all the same.' If they're whores, they're whores. They are what they are."

1: "Calm down, Don Hilario, not all that whorish. Sometimes we exaggerate. Your cousins, on the other hand . . . "

Somehow, I simply cannot develop a parallel between Don Hilario Cuernajón's cousins and the priest's daughters. Both of us are aware that the Spanish maid has come into the room, and we change the subject after a short silence, a bit stiffly, as if we had been caught in an ultrasecret conspiratorial conversation. And obviously Carmen has heard everything about the priest's daughters. I see by the flame in Picasso's eyes that he is gloating over the effect we have made on her.

"Would you like something to drink?" she asks.

"No thanks, Carmen."

When she leaves, we burst into laughter. "She must be scandalized," Don Hilario decides, and we go on talking about Navas de Malvivir.

Our conversation is interrupted for supper. This morning I had told Picasso I was returning to Rome in a few days, and he must suddenly have remembered it. He asks me pointblank:

"And what are you going to do in Rome?"

The abrupt questioning is just horseplay. He knows perfectly well that I live there. Influenced by the previous conversation, I say the first thing that comes into my head:

"I'm going to see the portrait of Innocent X. The only thing worth seeing in Rome, Don Hilario."

I am mistaken. Picasso has forgotten about Don Hilario Cuernajón and Navas de Malvivir. The image I have involuntarily brought to mind in mentioning the Velázquez painting is so strong that it immediately blots out our previous conversation.

"I don't know what people see in Velázquez," he says.

"But Pablo, the painting of Innocent X is marvelous," I blurt out, completely flabbergasted and unsure of myself.

"Well, I see nothing special in it. Velázquez! What does everybody see in Velázquez these days? I prefer El Greco a thousand times more. He was really a painter."

As always happens when I talk about painting with Picasso— and the reader will know exactly what I mean if he puts himself in my place—I cannot forget that the man I am talking to is Pablo Picasso. Yet despite everything, images bubble up in my spinning head: the Velázquez *Meninas*, a Le Nain I have seen frequently in the "secret room," and a Picasso quotation I vaguely recollect. For once, I answer without hesitation:

"What do you mean, Pablo? I read somewhere that you said Velázquez is better than Le Nain. I've also heard you say that Le Nain's *Wine Festival* is the eighth wonder of the world. And naturally I wonder why you are painting *Las Meninas*. I mean *your* Meninas. Or have I lost my mind?"

"No, you haven't lost your mind. But you must take certain things into account. First of all, I'm not always quoted correctly. Besides, sometimes I'm forced to say things I don't mean. It doesn't bother me, but that's another story. Secondly, we all have the right to change our minds, don't we? At least, I've changed mine many times—about painting and many other things."

This is beyond me. I could insist on the painting of Innocent X and ask him about Velázquez, but I can't find the words. It's better left the way it is. Picasso continues to ponder the matter, and after a long silence:

"Besides, there's another consideration, though it's difficult to express. How can I put it? I've also painted *Women of Algiers*,

A midnight visit to La Californie, the house Picasso lived in during the 1950s. In the background one can see a tapestry based on *Demoiselles d'Avignon*, Picasso's great masterpiece of 1907, which hangs in the Museum of Modern Art in New York.

with Delacroix in mind, who was thinking about Rubens when he painted the same subject. It occurred to me that maybe Delacroix didn't admire Rubens but liked to think he did. Do you understand?"

I understand. Naturally I understand.

This evening we are eating in the living room rather than the kitchen, where we usually eat. There are six of us around the only table, and there is scarcely any room for the dishes. Madame Leiris and Maurice Jardot are joking about insuring the works going to Paris and the impossibility of making a real evaluation "because the government of France would fall." More seriously, they estimate about thirty thousand dollars for every canvas, "just to make some sort of evaluation." In any case, there is no great problem, since the security measures taken will be in keeping with the value of the paintings. There will be a police escort for the trucks from Mougins to the Grand Palais, with a show of force worthy of an extraordinary bank operation. And police headquarters will follow the convoy of paintings by radio patrol during the entire trip. As if all this were not suf-

ficient, a representative from the Ministry will accompany the expert Louvre movers in one of the trucks.

Picasso listens to this talk with a mixture of curiosity and childlike admiration. It is as if he had personally unleashed a storm at sea by having accepted the homage show. But the details of the convoy do not hold his attention for very long, and he begins to tell me a lively story about André Breton, who has died several days ago in Paris.

"Seventy! And I thought he was much younger. Seventy! Of course, we forget that the years slip by for all of us. I still think of him as the young boy who invented all that about Surrealism."

He remembers that he knew Breton before the celebrated *Manifesto*, although he was not in Antibes, as some writer recorded it.

"I think it was the day before Apollinaire's death. I remember I was introduced to him in the passageway of Guillaume's house on the Boulevard Saint-Germain. Breton, a young man in uniform—a military doctor, I think—was extremely courteous. He talked about Apollinaire's health, and he couldn't conceal his grief."

Picasso speaks affectionately of the Surrealists, but without

Jacqueline and Maurice Jardot with the famous 1937 portrait of Dora Maar.

Jacqueline seen in profile with a front-view portrait of herself.

great enthusiasm. We talk for a long while about their ideas, especially hypnotic sleep and automatism. It strikes me as natural that the most meaningful theory for him in the whole Surrealist Weltanschauung is that of the poetic unconscious. I tell him so. He half agrees, but only seems satisfied when I tell him, in a somewhat joking yet basically serious manner:

"Very well. If you say no, automatism is not useful in painting. However, it seems to have been of some use to you in poetry. You're the only truly automatic poet, much more so than Breton in 1924. And as far as poetry is concerned, perhaps you *are* a Surrealist, despite yourself."

"Of course, of course. But that, too, has its explanation. I think we were all Surrealists, in a certain way, before the fashion. It was Apollinaire who invented the word, and he died in 1918. On the other hand, automatic writing is quite amusing. You know, I have the original manuscript of *L'Inmaculée Conception*, which Breton and Eluard wrote together, stored in some drawer here. Do you know the book? Well, the original is full of corrections. One can see just how automatic it all was."

After a while, the previous conversation is resumed. We speak of his "Surrealist" poetry, written in the 1930s.

"Some critics have said that I was affected by Surrealist

poetry, as well as by my family problems. Absolute nonsense. Basically I've always written the same way. And I've never stopped writing. Somewhere in the house there are dozens and dozens—what did I say?—hundreds and hundreds of poems that I've never published. Poems about the postman or the priest. In short, stories you already know."

As always, in his characteristic and curious style, a mixture of exaggeration and synthesis, he has hit the nail on the head. I think of the first poem in a book he gave me a few days before, *Dibujos y Estritos (8.1.59–19.1.59)*, published by Los Papeles de Son Armadans in Palma de Mallorca in 1961. I learned it by heart for his amusement:

> then came the postman later the tax-collector
> applause and *olés* and the blind man
> from the parish and the blackbird the
> daughters of Ramón and those of Doña
> Paquita the eldest a spinster
> and the clergyman all strange iciness
> painted in saffron and greens loaded
> with noodles and dark cotton grapes
> and fat bitter aloes and very
> perfect, well-ripened radishes and
> a frying pan round with eggs and potato
> and cowbells and the question over the shoulder
> rich and poor carried along by the storm
> over the wheat burning wet
> his hailstone shirt dirty clothes.

Some of Picasso's recent poems come to mind. Several of them are familiar from his having read them to me the summer before. It may be that the substance of his verse is, to quote one of his titles, "Absurdities." "My innate gift for automatic poetry— if this is what you mean by automatic poetry—is the same as it has always been, in the 30s, before the 30s, and now, when I write or when we tell our story about Navas de Malvivir."

But he has gone much further, spinning and weaving the thread of his thoughts:

"Besides, we Andalusians are a bit Surrealistic in any case. A good example is my uncle who wore a hairshirt; another was a bullfighter, you know, and perhaps the best, Don Luis de Góngora y Argote."

While we are having coffee, Jacqueline seems determined to put the finishing touches on our newly invented game.

"And if we all went to La Californie?" she asks, most innocently.

"But why should we go to La Californie? Aren't we all right here?"

"Of course, but that's not reason enough. What do you all think?"

84

A likeness of Toulouse-Lautrec on the mantelpiece gives the impression of a daguerreotype of a favorite ancestor.

"We'd be able to add a few more paintings for the exhibition. There's such a mass of paintings there. Surely you've forgotten something you'd like to send."

Picasso has caught the drift now and takes up his role again:

"Oh, no! That's enough! I don't want to hear any more about the exhibition."

Since we are all Jacqueline's accomplices and have agreed to go to La Californie after supper, Picasso decides: "It's just as well, I'll be able to go to bed in peace, etc. etc." All his opposition, however, does not prevent him from making his appearance at the door of the house, glowing, at the precise moment we are about to step into the automobiles. He is wearing a leather jacket slung over his shoulders and a tam-o'-shanter on his head. He announces, evidently to his own amazement, that he has not set foot in his house of the 1950s for five or six years, even though it is only a ten-minute drive from Notre Dame de Vie.

It is almost midnight when we awaken the caretakers at La Californie. A dachshund, one of a litter whelped while Picasso lived there, recognizes its master and leaps on him wildly. While Pablo stays in the garden playing with the animal, we enter the house. Packages of books, stacks of magazines, and several sculptures partially block our passage toward the main room.

We make our way in the dark, bumping into things. Jacqueline has disappeared to find the light switch. When the light finally goes on, it is blinding. The house looks as though it were still inhabited: furniture, paintings, photographs, magazines, more canvases, ceramics, books, letters, packages, dozens of packs of cigarettes and matches are strewn about in an "organized disorder." It is not too different from the main room at Notre Dame de Vie. In the adjoining dining room we discover a box of disintegrating Spanish sweets from 1960 and two bottles of sherry. One of them even has a corkscrew sunk into the cork.

Picasso makes his entrance like a whirlwind and walks directly to a strange piece of furniture, a dresser of sorts, in the passage between the dining and living rooms. He motions to me to join him.

"I want to show you something," he says, as he takes out a large but slender, carefully bound volume. "Look, this is a collection of André Breton's love letters. I bought them many years ago from the woman who received them, Breton's mistress, because I didn't want them to be hawked about and fall into just anyone's hands. I don't know how people can sell things like this."

We leaf through the originals and read some passionate paragraphs that have little in common with automatic poetry. They are more akin to the famous Breton poem, "Ma Femme":

Ma femme a la taille d'outre
entre les dents du tigre . . .

Turning a page, we see some peculiar stains that look as though drops of acid had fallen on the text, absorbing the ink.

"And what do you think this is? Guess!"

"Sulfuric acid," I venture.

"No, no. It's sperm." And, as he sees my disbelief, he adds:

"That's how Breton was. I told you before. A strange type. What an idea! Who would think of doing that? Not really a run-of-the-mill fellow—I told you."

Jacqueline and Mme Leiris repeat the "secret room" operation while Picasso and I wander from room to room. My attention is drawn to a striking miniature photograph at the edge of the mantel. It is a likeness of Toulouse-Lautrec surrounded by highly improbable objects, and it gives the impression of a daguerreotype of a favorite ancestor. Above the tiny Toulouse-Lautrec is a tapestry of *Les Demoiselles d'Avignon*, which seems to set the tone of the room. I ask Picasso to stand at the foot of "the girls," as we call them familiarly, so that I can make a photograph.

"Only your head will appear, in a corner," I tell him, for I see that "the girls" won't fit in the picture any other way.

"As if I were a signature."

"As if I were a signature," he answers unblinkingly.

In the silence that precedes the clicking of the shutter, we hear Jacqueline from the next room:

"Dora Maar, 1937 . . . 92 by 65 . . . Marie-Thérèse Walter, 61 by 46, 1937 . . . Jacqueline Roque, 1954 . . . 146 by 114 . . ."

*That* "girl" definitely has a sense of humor.

When we go out into the mild autumn night it is three o'clock, and the paintings at the Grand Palais, thanks to Jacqueline's inventiveness, will number not 60 or 80, but 116.

# CHAPTER 7

# Life at the Château

◀ Jacqueline cataloguing ceramics for the Paris show.

The last days of October, 1966

Three weeks later I return to Cannes for a few days, and visit Notre Dame de Vie daily. Actually, I am on my way to Paris for the inauguration of the famous homage exhibition. It will be divided among three locales: the Grand Palais, the Petit Palais, and the Bibliothèque National. My arrival at the château coincides with that of the trucks from the Louvre. They have come to pack up the pieces Picasso is lending for the exhibition. However, the picking and choosing of what is to go is still not finished. Jacqueline is bustling back and forth at a dizzying pace, separating the smaller pieces of sculpture and ceramics from the larger ones and classifying them carefully in one corner. She is adding still more pieces to the already enormous list which she conjured up in September.

One morning, while the Louvre people are hard at work loading the heavy sculptures into one of the trucks parked in the garden, Jacqueline invites us to La Californie. She wants to add several ceramics to the pieces going to Paris, even though the number of works seems to have reached saturation point. These ceramics are gathering dust somewhere in Picasso's previous residence. We go in two cars so that the pieces can be sent back to Notre Dame de Vie for cataloguing and wrapping as soon as possible. If we are quick, they can go in one of the trucks, which are almost ready to start for Paris.

The moment we reach La Californie, we go down to the half-basement, where several rooms are joined by a labyrinthine passage. They are low-ceilinged, and most of them are tiny. Despite the spaciousness of the upper floors, Picasso generally worked in one of these rooms. Now they are used for storage. One contains an ancient printing press. Picasso once began to experiment with printing his own graphics, but changed his mind when he realized how many complex technical procedures go into every edition of a print. But he continues to do the first, truly creative part of the edition, which is incising the metal or linoleum plates. During Picasso's years at La Californie, the master printer Jacques Frelaut printed his engravings on this ancient press. Frelaut would come from Paris whenever Picasso needed his help, and during those visits Picasso would drop the four other phases of his artistic life—painting, sculpture, drawing, and ceramics—to supervise the printing of each engraving. Now Aldo and Pierre Crommelynck, brothers who specialize in engraving, produce the editions for him in a small studio in Mougins.

Jacqueline sorts out the key for each room from a huge key-ring. We go into two rooms stacked with boxes and ceramics.

Once again we are amazed by her prodigious memory. She can put her hand on every forgotten painting, work of art, or even straight pin in Picasso's terrestrial kingdom. She goes straight to a fish painted in black, white, and red on an earth-colored background. She unwraps another plate, which shows a black-and-white owl. She decides not to take it because she remembers she already has a similar one at Notre Dame de Vie. She gathers up a couple of pitchers and hands them over to us. The last object we must unearth is an impressive bull's head, a bull with human eyes, in which green and jet black are the dominant tones. We now have more than twenty pieces, which we load into the minitruck. The chauffeur drives off slowly, well aware of the fragility and the immeasurable value of his cargo.

We go back into the house. Jacqueline decides to take a survey of some small sculptures which seem to have taken shape magi-

Jacqueline supervising the delicate job of wrapping the ceramics. At left she is with Aitana Alberti.

cally in the dusky shadows of the big main room. One of them is the famous head of a bull constructed from the handlebars and seat of a bicycle. For safety, I put it in my car trunk, wrapped in a couple of traveling blankets. Back at Notre Dame de Vie, someone unloads the trunk but does not realize that the head of the bull is under the blanket. As a result, I drive around the center of Cannes with the sculpture still in the car. When I discover the "bull" in the trunk, I return to the house, bring out the sculpture, and describe its itinerary.

"You're a fool," Picasso says. "You could have exchanged it for a real bicycle and nobody here would have been the wiser. Do you know how I happened to do this?" he continues, almost without taking a breath. "Well, I was with Sabartès on the way to someone's funeral and I saw this bicycle seat thrown into an empty lot. A little later, in another empty lot, I saw the handle-

Cathy unhesitatingly puts together
a complicated Picasso ceramic
without making a single mistake.

bars. It didn't occur to me all at once what I could do with
them, but I realized later that I was turning the matter over in
my head. As we left the cemetery I told Sabartès about them,
and we stopped to pick up the two parts. Curious, isn't it? I've
often felt like leaving this sculpture just anywhere. And it
wouldn't surprise me at all if someone found it and said: 'What
a nice head of a bull! You know, you could make a bicycle out of
it.'"

While I set the sculpture down in a corner of the studio, it
crosses my mind that this anecdote sums up Picasso's attitude
toward life and art, and even a curious aspect of his complex
thought process, better than any other statement. This thought
process achieves its most characteristic expression in paradox
and in a sense of humor that smacks of both the Spanish *pueblo*
and personal intuition. In a way, the game of creating a syn-

This sculpture, of which only a portion can be seen, is Picasso's famous study of a child jumping rope. Like many of Picasso's other sculptures, it was put together like a collage, using some rather unlikely elements, before being cast in bronze. The girl's body was fashioned from a basket.

thesis out of opposites is encompassed in this singular story, something of an obsession with the contrast between reality and fiction, between life and artistic creation. Of course, this is only one aspect of Picasso among many others. He is not easy to explain, and perhaps that is why so many hundreds of books on his life and work have been written without ever really plumbing the depths of the mystery.

The Louvre packers have finished with the sculptures and are now loading the paintings which were accumulated in the "secret room" early in October. Everyone is busy bringing canvases down to the sculpture room, where the specialists in delicate cargoes are gathering them to take out to the trucks. One of the packers, referring to his long experience in packing paintings, says to Picasso with natural pride:

Picasso chats with the Louvre packers. In the background, the plaster cast of a Michelangelo *Slave*.

"Don't worry, Maestro, I was with *La Gioconda* and *Venus* in Tokyo and New York."

Later that evening, Picasso repeats the boast and goes on to say:

"He talked about *La Gioconda* and *Venus* as if they were his girlfriends—how should I put it—as if they were whores. And as if that weren't enough, now he can use the same tone of voice and tell the next painter who has an homage show: "Don't worry, Maestro, I was with Picasso in the Petit and Grand Palais.""

The new gardener at Notre Dame de Vie and I are bringing an enormous canvas to the sculpture room. It is *La Cuisine*, a famous canvas painted in 1948. Halfway down the staircase, we scrape its edge at the angle where ceiling and wall meet. I am horrified to think we may have ruined part of a Picasso canvas, and in sight of the Maestro himself. Fortunately, he is down below talking with the packers, and only the rim of the stretcher has been touched. The other paintings are smaller and there are no further problems.

"Life at the château."

Someone makes an offhand remark about Pop art. Picasso, who has played only a small part in the selection of the works for Paris, suddenly shows an unusual interest in "two oval paintings." They have not yet been packed in the trucks.

"Where are they?" he asks Jacqueline. "The one with the pipe and glass—the playing-card one? And where's the other, the caned-chair one?"

Jacqueline knows at once. The first is going to the Petit Palais with the sculpture, because it is really an "object." It was painted in 1914, on wood, and its official title is *Verre, Pipe et Carte à Jouer*. This painting demonstrates, without a doubt, that Picasso is the grandfather of Pop, Op, and all their offshoots. The second is destined for the Grand Palais and will appear in the catalogue with a comment by the exhibition organizers that is worth noting: "The first example of collage (introduction onto the canvas of actual objects), preceding the invention of paper collages by Braque in 1912." Together with a small collection of similar sculptures, these two pieces will in a few weeks' time spark the admiration and interest of the public—as they do ours—by anticipating the latest modern artistic tendencies. Most especially *Construction au Gant*, done in 1930 with wood, canvas, sand, and glass, and which we are seeing today for the first time.

But just what is it that this man has invented? As if he is reading our minds, Picasso decides to act the simpleton, but his eyes glisten with malice and just a trace of smugness.

Our only duty now is to wrap the ceramics. To save time, Jacqueline decides on a very efficient way to catalogue them. Using an old-fashioned box camera, she photographs each piece in the garden just before it is taken to the sculpture room for wrapping. Then she supervises the meticulous work of the packers, who are busily rolling each ceramic in a protective straw blanket.

When the light begins to fail, we have an aperitif with the people from the Louvre in the sculpture room. Tomorrow the packers will leave with the treasure trove, protected by a tight police escort. As he stretches long strips of adhesive tape across the glass on some of the paintings, one of the packers, who has already amused Picasso with his conversation, remarks seriously:

"Oh well. That's life at the château!"

The phrase becomes a durable household catchphrase for almost any situation.

"Life at the château!" Actually, the phrase is only valid for someone who is on the outside looking in, dazzled by the deceptive exterior of Notre Dame de Vie. For the Master of the

Castle, on the other hand, "life at the château" means working like a monster with twelve arms from the moment he wakens until he goes to bed. The only interruptions consist of meals and the time which friends and strangers "miserably" rob from him. Yet, thinking it over, there was a grain of truth in that phrase. Had it not been for Picasso's one and only experience with surgery a while ago—it will be a year exactly on the day the Paris exhibition opens—he would never have known such a long period of idleness. "Life at the château," even if he did not know it himself, is this period in 1966 which is now drawing to a close. The Master of Mougins has already begun intense drawing sessions, and soon he will be painting one or two canvases a day, as in his most productive periods.

The trucks leave at eleven in the morning. Picasso watches them from his bedroom terrace as they fade into the distance. When I go up to join him I ask a question to which I already know the answer.

"Am I going to Paris? Oh, no. Look, what do I have to do in Paris? Besides, I'm horrified at homage shows. Not only now, but ever since Málaga, when I was to be awarded a medal and didn't even show up. I don't know if it embarrasses me or something like that. I just don't know."

He is enormously shy, though the fact is not immediately apparent because of his flippancy about so many things. In fact, he is so shy that he becomes slightly annoyed at having to talk about the show any more and quickly changes the subject:

"And the sculpture of the man with the sheep?" he asks.

Automatically I look down at the place the sculpture normally occupies in the garden.

"What a fool I am," Picasso goes on. "They just took it with them a moment ago. You laugh, but these things happen, just like asking a widow about her freshly buried husband. The worst part is that I'm going to miss the man with the sheep. I'm so used to pissing on it from the first-floor studio."

As if we had never spoken of it before, he describes the value of urine in developing a really handsome patina on bronze. He is so disconcerted by the commotion of the trucks' departure that he forgets he has already described this process to me. His loss of memory seems to me the result of an attack of shyness.

Speech as well as memory. At supper Picasso appears a million miles off, lost in thought and profoundly quiet. Surely he is thinking of the exhibition. When he can no longer bear it or keep it to himself, he says quite suddenly:

"I really don't know why I let it happen. Basically, I'm against exhibitions and homages, as you know. Moreover, it is of no use to anyone. Painting, exhibiting—what's it all about?"

Picasso, Jacqueline, and Louise Leiris in the sculpture room. On the stool in front of the Michelangelo *Slave* is *Woman from Chicago*.

We are all thunderstruck and do not know what to say. After a few moments, which seem endless, someone remarks playfully, as if to cut short Picasso's somber monologue:

"If you like, I'll go to Paris, to the Grand Palais, and slash all your paintings."

"It's not that either. Do you know what I mean? It's not a matter of slashing the paintings or destroying them, but neither did I have to say yes to the exhibition. None of you understand a thing. All this business about homages is ridiculous. What's the use of it all? Who really cares about what I paint?"

He leaves the meal in the same dispirited mood, with the same thing on his mind. I am quite sure he felt very much the same way at his first showing, at Ambroise Vollard's gallery sixty-five years ago.

# CHAPTER 8

# "Let's Dance"

◄ Picasso says goodbye to the Louvre people and several hundred creatures of his imagination.

Today Picasso is going for an outing with four Spanish friends. He is only beginning to get about again since his operation. A few days earlier he had gone to visit his lifelong friend, the Russian writer Ilya Ehrenburg, who had sent word to Picasso that he was on the Riviera. Ehrenburg had had little hope of seeing Picasso, and told us a couple of years later in Rome just how surprised he was when Picasso appeared that day, "quite thin but with an even more intense expression than before."

"I was certain I wouldn't see him, because I knew he had been ill and was convalescing. But didn't the Devil himself show up at my hotel in Menton! I think I'm right in calling him the Devil—*Tchort* in Russian. The Devil has the gift of divination, among other things, as everyone knows. And Picasso must have guessed how badly I needed to see him. Just before the operation he had been awarded the Lenin Prize, and the Russian ambassador in Paris had telephoned Notre Dame de Vie to ask when he could deliver it in person. He was told to come the following Thursday. When the ambassador arrived at the door of the house, he was told that Picasso had gone on a trip. Needless to say, it caused a terrible upheaval in Moscow. A few months later they sent me to see if I couldn't somehow patch things up, since I happened to be the only personal friend of Picasso's in the Soviet Union. Well, he did come to see me in Menton, and I took out the medal that goes with the prize. I realized that I had better talk to him in a way he could understand, so I said: 'Look here, Pablo, take the medal. Do what you like with it, keep it in a drawer or hang it around your afghan's neck, but for heaven's sake take it, or I'm not going back to Moscow. O.K.?' He took the medal quite solemnly, put it in his pocket, and then we embraced, roaring with laughter."

Picasso's version of the same anecdote is noteworthy for its brevity and concentration on one detail:

"He wanted to put the Lenin Prize on my dog. What a lunatic!"

Picasso has decided to take his four friends to the ceramic studio at Vallauris. Before they drive down the little street that leads to the studio, he has the car stop in front of a barbershop in the busy downtown area. He wants to introduce his friends to another Spaniard in exile—as they themselves are—to Enrique Arias, from Buitrago de Lozoya.

Arias is a small man with a roguish expression in his eyes. His quick native intelligence is very much that of the rural Castillian. He has been a good friend of Picasso's for more than

twenty years, since the artist began frequenting Vallauris.
Arias's most prized possessions are a wooden box decorated by
Picasso with a bullfight scene, and a curious drawing of a huge
bird, engraved on a metal plate, which he uses to adorn his
business quarters. He stores his barbering equipment in the box,
carrying it with him when he goes to Notre Dame de Vie to cut
the hair of his more renowned compatriot. This happens every
ten or fifteen days, not because Picasso's hair grows abnormally
fast, but because both Picasso and Arias are always eager to
talk about their favorite subject. While Arias plies his scissors,
they talk endlessly about the *corrida*—the previous season, the
one coming up, the latest bullfight news they have culled from
the ABC—or simply about the state of affairs this year in Spain.

After having discussed all these matters and a thousand more
with Arias and the other Spaniards, Picasso invites the four to
leave the barbershop "so Arias can get back to his clients." But
the habitués of the shop seem to accept these sudden appear-
ances of Picasso as the most natural of village events. They do
not say a word, but just sit patiently on the barber chairs, white
bibs tied around their necks, until the Maestro decides to take
his leave.

As we cross the street, a man rushes toward Picasso with a
shout of joy, his arms spread wide. It is Serge Lifar, the famous
Russian dancer.

"What a coincidence, Pablo!" He is obviously thrilled. "It's

Picasso meets Serge Lifar, dancer and choreographer, and Mrs. Lifar on a street in Vallauris. Together they improvise a few ballet steps.

been years since I've been in Vallauris, and the first person I bump into as I get out of the car is no other than you."

Lifar joins the small group around Picasso and walks as far as the entrance to the ceramics studio. Holding Picasso by the arm, he talks without a second's pause. He mentions Diaghilev, the Princess de Polignac, Coco Chanel, Erik Satie, and many others formerly connected with the celebrated Russian ballets of the "belle époque." These dazzling names alternate with the equally dazzling titles of five or six ballets of which Lifar was either star or choreographer and Picasso was set designer or simply a spectator. Between snapping one picture and another I catch a reference to *Train Bleu,* which was famous in 1923, and also *Icare,* the ballet for which Picasso designed his last theater curtain in 1960. Picasso keeps nodding, not saying a word but smiling happily.

"Do you remember, Pablo? I used to do it like this."

And Lifar suddenly leaps into a ballet stance, with impeccable form for a dancer who has already turned sixty. Picasso offers his hand to balance him as he turns slowly, and then stretches out his arm to give him room to execute some spectacular pirouettes. But, to tell the truth, as an extemporaneous ballet dancer—at eighty-five!—maintaining the right distances and timing, Picasso gives an even better performance.

# CHAPTER 9

# Far from Spain

Picasso's devotion to poetry has been well known ever since that day in 1904 when he wrote "Au rendez-vous des poètes" on the door of his modest Montmartre studio. Nor is it a secret that one of the most significant elements of his life has been his close association with poets. Guillaume Apollinaire, Max Jacob, André Salmon, Paul Eluard, Jean Cocteau, Tristan Tzara, Pierre Reverdy, and others no less revered in the world of poetry are among those with whom Picasso has maintained his greatest friendships. As Picasso recalls it, it was Rafaël Alberti, a young vanguard poet in the 1930s, to whom he first read his own poetry. From then on, a deep mutual respect bound them together.

20 February 1968

Picasso and his old friend have been holding forth for the last two hours. The conversation is both lighthearted and down to earth. They are discussing Andalusia, bulls and bullfighters, popular and folk songs, Alberti's cousins, Picasso's aunts and uncles. The rest of us listen silently, captivated by the spellbinding gestures and endless verbal creativity that seem to come so naturally to these two Andalusians. Suddenly they seem weary of frivolity and begin to talk seriously. But this impression turns out to be mistaken:

ALBERTI: "Do you know what I was thinking about while I strolled along the port here in Antibes? That the people in your paintings suddenly seem to be walking around all over the place. People with an eye in their elbow, others with two noses, one with a breast growing out of her shoulder."

PICASSO: "Of course there are."

ALBERTI: "I'm convinced painters create a certain type of real person over the years. I'm sure Goya never saw flesh-and-blood types such as he painted, but today Spain is full of them."

PICASSO: "That's absolutely true. Painters create people who eventually become a reality. Naturally, Goya couldn't see the characters he painted, for they weren't alive during his lifetime. Yet Spain is full of them now, as you say. For example, something awful happened to me in Royan when the war broke out. I went out into the street and who's the first person I see? A little girl, the spitting image of the little girl in the painting I had just been working on. You can't imagine the terror I felt."

23 February 1968

Picasso has just received a copy of a Spanish magazine with reproductions of paintings done by his cousin Manuel Blanco,

◀ Picasso in his most recent studio, chatting with his good friend, the Spanish poet Rafaël Alberti. The studio had been a terrace, which the artist enclosed in 1964 "because I no longer have room to paint in. The house is full of paintings, everywhere. They breed like rabbits!"

Picasso enjoys listening to Alberti tell an outlandish story.

a primitive artist who keeps painting his famous relative. They are simple family cutouts, reminiscent of old daguerreotypes. Though they have a certain charm, they forever sound the same refrain: "Pablo Picasso with His Cousin Fulano," "Picasso's Family in Such-and-Such a Room . . ."

The magazine sends Picasso in search of an album from the Málaga Museum, which he leafs through, entertained and delighted, in Alberti's company. At the end there is an early Picasso still life, a painting of a ceramic jug and a bowl of fruit.

PICASSO: "I remember that painting as if I had done it yesterday. Do you see the grapes? While I was painting, I ate all the ones on the other side, the side that doesn't show in the painting. In other words, the only grapes left are the ones you see. In a certain sense it was a Herculean task to arrange this bunch of grapes so that I could paint them as if I hadn't eaten a good half of them."


Occasionally they bring up the subject of the Prado Museum, rehashing a hypothetical problem we have all heard several times with the slightest of variations:

PICASSO: "What do you mean, what if I had decided to go to the Prado? How can you even imagine such a thing, Rafaël! God, no! The truth is that I did go there a few times to visit my friend Bernereggi, an Argentinian of about my own age who was copying Goyas and other famous paintings."

After a rather majestic pause, he continues in a casual tone of voice:

PICASSO: "However, the Prado and I do have something in common, as you know. I was one of its directors in the days of the Republic, when I was nominated and elected its chief. Actually, I still am, since no one has bothered to fire me."

The situation is very amusing, for we all know that Alberti himself had a good bit to do with Picasso's appointment. But the poet takes up his role with the poker-faced seriousness it demands.

ALBERTI: "And what would you do if you went back and took over your appointment?"

PICASSO: "What would I do? I'd keep all the frames—they're fabulous—and leave everything else for them to do with as they pleased."


During the evening, the conversation turns to Picasso's most famous painting, *Guernica*. Should it or should it not be returned to Spain? Are the students and professors right in petitioning the Madrid government to ask Picasso to take the painting back from the Museum of Modern Art in New York, where it is on loan, and return it to Spain?

Since childhood Picasso has kept an intimate "diary" of
drawings. Here he shows Alberti the first notebook he has
finished since his operation.

PICASSO: "No, absolutely not. I couldn't agree with them less. You see, those same students who want *Guernica* in Spain don't really know if what they're doing is good or bad. The proof is that they've written me a long letter asking my opinion, because they aren't sure."

Pilar, a Spanish friend who is also visiting, says the painting "must be returned to Spain right now, since Spain is where it belongs." Alberti, on the other hand, clarifies two distinct aspects of the situation. One is that the students are doing quite well in using their demand as a weapon in the political struggle. The other is summed up in his argument that *Guernica* "must not be returned to Spain now, because it would be a victory for the regime, with its pretense of democratic leanings."

PICASSO: "That's it. The painting belongs to the Republican government and not to Franco's."

ALBERTI: "In any case, all of this is beside the point. Suppose you acted on the students' petition and decided that the painting should be returned to Spain on condition it be hung in the Prado. Now let us put ourselves in the position of the Franco government. They'd never accept. They couldn't. It would be like asking a murderer to produce the body of his victim for purposes of exhibition."

Picasso takes a fancy to this observation:

"The truth of the matter is that by means of *Guernica* I have the pleasure of making a political statement every day in the middle of New York City. No one else can do that. Anyway, what do I know about all this? Only that no minister or politician could do as much."

After a brief pause:

"No, for the moment it is just right where it is. Naturally, someday it will have to be returned to Spain. Because *Guernica,* as everyone knows, *is* the Spanish people."

Trying to decipher a forgotten Cubist drawing.

# CHAPTER 10

# The Endless Catalogue

Picasso is working with Christian Zervos in the main room at Notre Dame de Vie. The distinguished critic and editor of *Cahiers d'Art* is preparing Volume 19 of his monumental catalogue of Picasso's work. Some 4,500 unpublished drawings from the painter's private collection have just been photographed. The photographs they are looking at now, however, are destined not for Volume 19 but for a supplement covering Picasso's Cubist period. There are literally dozens more, of drawings made from 1910 on, which Zervos has gathered with infinite patience. Together, Picasso and Zervos are trying to date them and to see whether Picasso can remember what each of them "signifies."

ZERVOS: "Do you remember this one?"

PICASSO, after examining the photo carefully, says slowly: "I don't remember it. No. I don't know."

He looks at the photo once more and hands it to me.

PICASSO: "I don't see anything, do you?"

I examine the photo. I must admit that I can only make out a mass of rectangles, semicircles, and superimposed cubes. I return the photo to Zervos.

PICASSO: "And you, Zervos. You see nothing in it?"

ZERVOS: "No. I see nothing."

The scene is repeated several times. Picasso is now contemplating the photo of this drawing for the fourth time and is about to admit defeat. Suddenly, his eyes begin to glow.

PICASSO: "I know. Now I know. They're boxers. Do you see?"

And we *do* see. As if by magic, two boxers emerge from the interlaced rhomboids and cubes. Their fists are raised high, about to smash in each other's faces.

30 September 1966

Zervos and Picasso are in the same place again, still cataloguing Cubist drawings. Picasso occasionally stops working, leaving Zervos on tenterhooks. He sips a huge cup of "Queen of the Fields," an herb tea ordered by his doctors (the name amuses him enormously). Or he takes a break to start a conversation with me, usually by evoking one or another nostalgic recollection.

ZERVOS: "What's the date of this one?"

PICASSO: "I don't know."

ZERVOS: "You don't have any idea?"

"It's a fake," Picasso says.
"Obviously. It's *so* bad," Christian
Zervos replies.

PICASSO: "No. Look, how do you expect me to remember?"

Silence. The photo is passed back and forth. From a distance it looks as if a poker game is going on, with cards being dealt, shuffled, and passed back and forth.

ZERVOS: "Perhaps 1912?"

PICASSO: "Yes. Okay. That'll do. Make it 1912."

And turning to me, he says:

"1912, 1913, 1914, it's all the same. The funny part comes later, when Zervos puts down 1912 and everybody says it's 1912. For all I know it's 1915."

1 October 1966

Zervos shows us some photos of portrait drawings from the 1920s. They are done in bold strokes, in ink or pencil, and are similar to the well-known ones of Manuel de Falla and Stravinsky. They especially remind me of another portrait from this same period, that of the Chilean poet Vicente Huidobro, which I have seen somewhere or other. I tell Picasso this.

PICASSO: "Oh yes, that's true. Do you know it, Zervos?"

ZERVOS, interested: "No. I never saw it."

I: "Well, I think I saw it reproduced on the first page of one of his anthologies that was published by Zig-Zag about twenty years ago in Chile."

PICASSO: "You'd better write that down, Zervos. Maybe you can track it down."

Between photos, Picasso and I go on talking about South American poets, especially Vallejo and Huidobro. But mostly we discuss some lesser-known poets and writers from the days of *Arte Joven,* the magazine Picasso founded with Francisco Soler in Madrid around 1901. It is all but forgotten now. Picasso becomes tenderly nostalgic and talkative as he recalls Pedro Barrantes, Camilo Bargicla, Alberto Lozano, and Enrique Cornuti.

"Cornuti was French, from Beziers," he comments, with his usual obsession for detail, "and he spoke awful Spanish. But he was the one who taught all those people in Madrid what they needed to know about French poetry and a lot of other things besides. He was a real nut. He went to a cemetery with me one night—one of those crazy stunts we indulged ourselves in during those days—and he proceeded to declaim reams of poetry among the tombstones."

I realize that my presence is distracting them from their work and leave quietly, taking refuge in "Jacqueline's little house," which is some forty feet from the main house. I sit down in front of the fireplace and start reading the first book that comes to hand from Jacqueline's library. But before I can read

Year after year, the photographers Zervos brings with him
record Picasso's prodigious output. "It's like going to the
movies—or to a bullfight," the artist says.

more than a couple of pages, Zervos appears at the door holding
a photo:

"Pablo sent me to ask you who this is. He seems to be a
Mexican poet, or someone like that. You're supposed to be a
great expert on South American poets, after what you said
about the portrait of Huidobro."

That such a thought should cross Picasso's mind causes us a
moment of hilarity. We conclude that Picasso has definitely lost
interest in cataloguing drawings, and is prepared to invent
any excuse to dawdle away the day and night.

Jacqueline follows the photographers' progress. At one
point she quietly disappears and returns with another canvas
from the same period.

Opposite page: One of Picasso's favorite themes—the painter at his easel. Right: The painting on the easel, from May 1962, was the embryonic idea that later developed into *Woman from Chicago.*

## 15 February 1968

More than a year has gone by since the previous gathering. Now Zervos is photographing Picasso's paintings from the years between 1956 and 1963 for Volume 20 of the endless catalogue. The two photographers who have come with him are setting the canvases on the large easel. If the paintings are very small, as sometimes happens with "heads," they photograph two at a time. Each picture requires a series of meticulous procedures: measuring the canvas, numbering it, adjusting the distance between the terribly heavy camera and the painting, checking and controlling the lighting, noting all the necessary details in a notebook, not moving a muscle while the shutter is clicked, and so forth.

Picasso, seated in the dark on an old sofa, is watching the

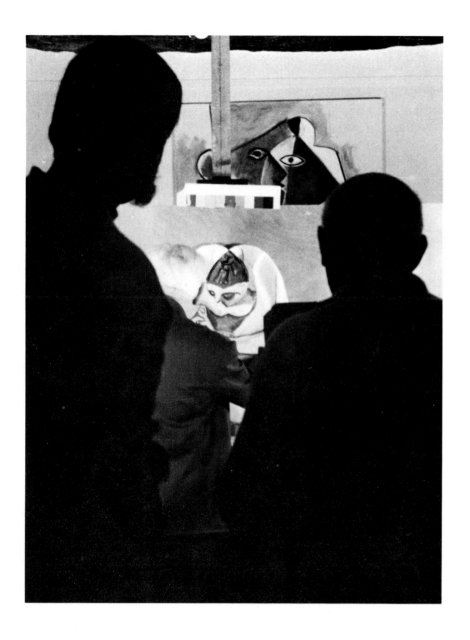

Zervos moves back and forth, not missing the slightest detail of the photographers' work.

photographers at work. "It's like going to the movies—or to a bullfight," he remarks later. Jacqueline and Mme Zervos are helping in the "photographic operation." Jacqueline selects the paintings on the first floor and then brings them downstairs, whereupon Mme Zervos notes the data in a school notebook. Sometimes she sits down on a long narrow bench to avoid being blinded by the light from the two lamps.

ZERVOS: "You know, I finally discovered who that Mexican poet of last year is. Anyway, he's not a Mexican, he's Venezuelan. He still lives in Paris, and his name is Ganso."

As Zervos gets up to take a close look at a work painted on

A portrait of the poet Jacques Prevert, with the eternal cigarette between his lips.

wood, which has just been set up on the easel, I stare at him in silent admiration. In view of such perseverance, like that of a bloodhound hot on a trail, it is not surprising that his catalogue has become an indispensable guide to the century's most important artistic achievement.

A small canvas dated 26 July 1957 is put on the easel to be photographed. It is a vine leaf, barely sketched in and covered with peculiar spots. On closer observation we see that there is not only paint on the leaf, but also seed—real birdseed, probably—glued to the canvas.

PICASSO: "Yes, that's what it is. When I did it I was thinking of that Greek story—what was it called—anyway, it was about the birds coming and eating."

ZERVOS, who is in another part of the room, has picked up Picasso's idea out of the air, despite the distance: "You mean Apelles."

134

An Imaginary Personage painted early in 1968.

PICASSO: "That's right. Apelles. That day I wanted to work like Apelles."

ZERVOS: "Yes, but it isn't really the same thing. Apelles drew the grapes and the birds were fooled by the drawing. But you used a trick."

PICASSO: "That's true. You're right. Still, basically it's the same thing, isn't it?"

28 February 1968

Today Zervos is photographing Picasso's latest paintings. Almost all of them are rather large portraits of imaginary people. Some are actually quite recent, according to the dates drawn in with enormous numbers and letters. There are some magnificent ones dating from the third to the sixth of this month, that is, from only a few weeks ago, and we realize that Picasso has been painting at the rate of two canvases a day. This reminds

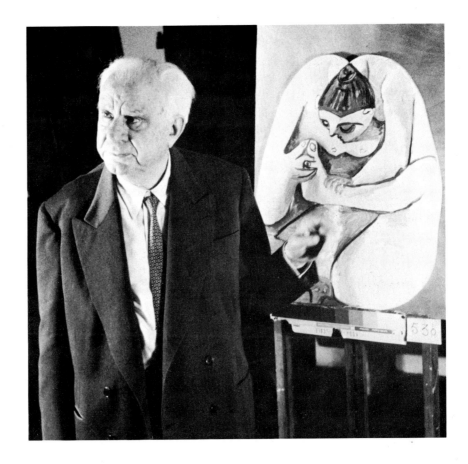

Opposite page: Above, Zervos chats with Jacqueline; below, an Imaginary Personage takes her turn on the easel. Right: "I'd also like to do a catalogue of fake 'Picassos,'" Zervos says.

us, much to Picasso's amusement, of that most alarming criticism printed in France on the occasion of his first Paris show: "He's only twenty," Félicien Fagusek wrote, "and paints as many as three canvases a day."

Between one painting and another I ask Zervos how many "Picassos" he has photographed from the time he started putting together his catalogue in 1932.

ZERVOS: "More than twenty thousand items."

I: "And how many more are missing?"

ZERVOS: "An immense number. If Picasso should decide today to stop painting, which as you know is totally impossible, I would still have to produce some ten thousand more items."

He goes on to say: I'd also like to do a catalogue of fake 'Picassos.'" Hundreds upon hundreds have passed through his hands, both "original" fakes and photographs.

ZERVOS: "However, when I think about it seriously, I simply can't work up any enthusiasm for the idea. In general, the fakes are so very bad."

He also tells me that the various "schools" which specialize in fake "Picassos" could be a field of study in themselves:

"For example, during the war an absolute avalanche of

137

Jacqueline has just
brought in a forgotten painting
from the "little" house at Notre
Dame de Vie. Right: Yvonne
Zervos records the relevant data
about each painting.

apocryphal "Picassos" were turned out in England. Before the
war they all came from Barcelona, and were really awful.
They are back to doing them in Barcelona now, somewhat
better, if one can put it that way. I receive an average of two
or three a day. These painters of fakes obviously have no other
motive than a desire to see themselves immortalized in my
catalogue one of these days."

[Zervos died in 1971, and the last volume, number 26, on
which he was then working, appeared in 1972, thirty years
after the first volume.]

That evening Zervos shows us, without comment, two photos
of a drawing of *L'Homme au Mouton*. Actually, he suspects their
authenticity. Picasso scarcely glances at them and says unhesitatingly:

"It's a fake."

138

ZERVOS: "Obviously. It's *so* bad! As if the upper part of one real 'Picasso' had been glued to the lower part of another. One can see that from a distance."

Picasso writes "fake" on the back of each photograph. As on other occasions, the speed with which he reaches a decision astonishes me. A glance suffices.

When the last photograph has been examined, the subject turns to fakes in general. Picasso says that a good look at the eyes of the inhabitants of a Douanier Rousseau is enough to establish its authenticity. "That's the secret," he concludes, and bids us goodnight, without, however, revealing what detail distinguishes a fake "Picasso" from a real one.

"Oh, that's *far* more complicated," he says with a roguish smile. We say goodnight again and leave him alone with his secret, under the ancient olive tree which stands guard over the entrance of Notre Dame de Vie.

Imaginary Personages painted early in 1968. These were the first in a long series which Picasso works on until his death. With infinite variations, the works of his last period, from 1968 to 1973, show fantastic creatures, each pathetically isolated from any context in the solitude of its canvas.

The paint is still wet on this canvas as it is being photographed.

The paintings are sometimes placed sideways in order to fit them into camera range. Opposite page: As one can see from the roman numeral IV after the date, Picasso has not slowed down since 1901, when he arrived in Paris and an art critic wrote: "He's only twenty, and paints as many as three canvases a day."

"There are few girls like that anymore," Picasso says when this painting appears on the easel.

A corner of the studio. The photograph shows Picasso with his magnificent Afghan hound, Kaboul.

◀ Picasso dedicates catalogues of the "Twenty Years of Ceramics" exhibition for the staff at the Galería Madoura.

A corner of the main room at Notre Dame de Vie. The television set is seldom turned on, but at one point Picasso enjoyed watching wrestling matches. The painting is of the harbor at Cannes, which Picasso can see from his balcony. The ceramic-tile mosaic beneath it shows an Imaginary Personage; the small face in its lower right corner is probably a happy but chance replacement of a broken tile.

The couch in the main room is forever packed to overflowing
with the unlikeliest objects. The *Minotaur* at the right is an
original collage; the other pictures are reproductions of Picasso
paintings. At the left of this extraordinary labyrinth is a
photograph of a little boy, Pablo, Diego, José, Francisco de
Paula, Juan Nepumuceno, María de los Remedios, Cipriano de
la Santísima Trinidad Ruiz Picasso. Seven first names and two
last names—such a collection could belong to a nobleman or to
any ordinary gypsy.

The artist in his bedroom, inscribing a book that has just been published about him.

Picasso and Jacqueline in the main room. He has just received
the first catalogues of the ceramics exhibition.

Picasso and Jacqueline with Kaboul on the patio at Notre Dame de Vie.

# Part II

# CONVERSATIONS

Pablo Ruiz Picasso's last family.

18 May 1965

PICASSO: "Age. Experience. I don't believe in any of that. Every time I hear someone talk about age and experience, I can't help thinking of something Satie once said: 'During the course of my entire life, I've heard it solemnly declared that "When you're fifty, you'll see. Then you'll see." However, I turned fifty a long time ago, and I have yet to see anything.'"

The mere mention of Satie, the great composer of *Parade*, brings some anecdotes to Picasso's mind, amusing anecdotes as always, since they deal with an extraordinary person, the very prototype of the "belle époque" bohemian.

"Satie was very funny. One day Princess Polignac, who was a Maecenas, among other things, got wind of the fact that our friend was in financial straits, so she sent him a thousand francs to tide him over the crisis. Now, a thousand francs in those days was a good

chunk of money. And do you know what that barbarian Satie did? He sent her a card with these words: 'My poor lady, you can believe me when I assure you that your thousand francs have not fallen on deaf ears. Erik Satie.' Can you imagine! Calling the princess 'My poor lady.'"

17 June 1965

Could the story Picasso is telling today possibly be true?

"I despise wasting my time with people. Not only now, but ever since I can remember. A long time ago, when I was living up there in Montmartre, more dead than alive with hunger, I had a visit from some Germans who said they were great admirers. They had even bought one of my paintings. A good friend of mine was with them, Wilhelm Uhde, and he also had bought one of my paintings. They invited me out and proceeded to wine and dine

Picasso in his last studio.

me. Naturally, the night wore on and it was getting late. They were so busy flattering me, telling me how much they liked me and how they couldn't let me return to my studio, that I finally had to say: 'Is that so? Now, we'll just find out if that's true or not.' I took out my revolver, which I always carried with me, and fired several shots into the walls. They took their leave quickly enough then, frightened out of their wits, but at last I was alone—and that was what I wanted."

Whether or not shots were really fired that night, the revolver did exist. By chance, rereading a well-known biography of Picasso this very afternoon, I come across a remark made by Berthe Weill, who bought three Picasso paintings in 1901: "He holds a revolver to your head and demands money."

Some time later, upon reading Hubert Fabureau's biography of the poet Max Jacob, I become totally convinced that Picasso was telling the truth, and I regret my unpardona-ble lack of trust in his "seriousness." Fabureau's biography, published in 1935, during Jacob's lifetime, contains the following anecdote: "To titillate the neighborhood, Picasso fires his revolver. It is a gift from Alfred Jarry, and he enjoys it. When someone speaks of Cézanne in a tone that displeases Picasso, he says: 'One more word and I shoot!' But at the same time he lays the gun, which he always carries, on the table."

18 June 1965

Picasso goes on telling stories about the days when he was living "up there."

PICASSO: "You can't imagine how terrible it is not to have money. I'll never forget what happened to me once with a very rich man—whose name I would rather not recall —just after I set up my Bateau-Lavoir studio. He came to see my paintings. After having looked everything over, he sat down on a

158

rocking chair and stayed a long time, rocking back and forth. Finally he selected a painting and threw the money for it over his shoulder, without so much as standing up."

"And what did you do?"

"What did I do? I picked up the money and put it in my pocket. For me, it was more important to work. Do you know what I mean? Work has always been the one constant in my life. But as you can see, neither have I been able to forget the incident."

8 July 1965

PICASSO: "Does it always rain in Rome?"

I: "That depends. It's fairly rainy in winter. Why do you ask?"

PICASSO: "Because I remember it rained buckets when I was there with Diaghilev's ballet. One day I had to slap Cocteau across the face because of the rain."

The tone of his voice makes it quite clear that he is absolutely serious.

PICASSO: "As I said, it was pouring. We had to go to the house of one of Cocteau's fancy friends, a countess or something like that. We couldn't get a cab anywhere—naturally they were horse-drawn cabs—and Cocteau became so upset and nervous, since we obviously were going to be late, that he had a hysterical fit. I had to smack him a couple of times to calm him down."

15 August 1966

Nine months have passed since Picasso's operation. His recovery has been remarkably swift. Even the doctors are astounded. And his improvement has been especially noticeable during this past week. Not only has he worked longer hours than usual, but he has felt like going out. Yesterday we went to the bullfight, and today we're at the beach.

When the attendants at the bathing place see him coming, they leave their other clients temporarily and flutter about us like homing

Picasso in his bedroom, dedicating a ceramic and a book.

pigeons, bringing an assortment of beach umbrellas, deck chairs, air mattresses, and tiny tables. Then they set up the barriers which indicate the area reserved for each umbrella. To celebrate the return of the house favorite, they bring a bottle of champagne. And, most important, they discreetly keep the curiosity seekers, the autograph hunters, and the Sunday photographers at bay.

Picasso is wearing a wide-brimmed beach hat. Someone in our group begins a song to suit the occasion, and, recognizing the words, Picasso repeats the refrain:

When I'm off to the bullfight in Jerez
I sport my hat with proud flamboyance
At every step there's a hum of *olés*
The *toreros* aren't applauded half as much as
    I am.

We go into the water. Picasso pretends to be a marvelous swimmer, but actually he only knows how to float and splash about a bit along the shore. Still, the imitation is so realistic that from a distance nobody could tell if his "swimming" is authentic or not. Jacqueline has left us and has swum far out.

PICASSO: "I could swim as far as Jacqueline if I wanted to. But why should I?"

He goes back to floating. Suddenly he stands up and points to the jetty at Cannes, which is outlined in the bright Mediterranean light half a mile or so from where we are. The silhouettes of the people strolling back and forth from the lighthouse are amazingly clear and sharp. The sun is shimmering before our eyes, exploding the wharf into a million moving luminous points.

"It's fantastic," Picasso says, with an unusual show of joy, "they really do look like tiny ants."

It certainly is fantastic. And also a pity. Because if he were not in water up to his chest, and had paper and pencil in hand, it would perhaps be the beginnings of a new "series."

12 December 1966

I have just returned from Paris, where I have seen the "Hommage à Picasso" exhibition. It is the most comprehensive showing of his work ever mounted. He is less excited than he was the last time I saw him, when the Louvre trucks were leaving, but somewhat more on edge than usual. He goes to the heart of the matter immediately:

"How was it? Tell me. Tell me everything."

Since I know full well that other visitors have already raved to him about this enormous show and that he has also read the critics and their eulogies in the newspapers, I decide to say something totally nonsensical:

"Absolutely hideous."

"Ah, yes? I said it would be. You see, Jacqueline? At last the truth is out about this whole Paris business. I told you this would happen."

A short pause and I go on:

"First of all, the paintings were too close together."

"You see? Do you see how right he is? It looked that way to me from a photo I saw in a magazine."

"Besides, there are a lot of paintings hung upside down."

"What a mess! I knew it would be like that."

The truth is I did see one painting hung upside down, but the joke is going so well it seems a pity to let it drop. He takes the catalogue from the table and looks for the painting in question. Finally I have to find it for him. It is *Guitarre*, a collage done with cloth, string, nails, and paper, and dated 1926.

"You're right."

"Don't worry. It's the only one."

Picasso, who had understood from the first that we were half joking, answers without a second's hesitation:

"You're wrong. There's another one."

And he goes through the voluminous

At a waterfront restaurant in Cannes in 1960 with Camilo José Cela, the Spanish novelist, and poet Anthony Kerrigan (across from Picasso).

catalogue for a long time without finding one. In the end he goes back to *Guitarre* and draws some arrows on either side of the photographic reproduction—also upside down—to indicate "how it must be seen." He turns back to the first page and dedicates the catalogue, as is his custom, and adds a little drawing.

"Take it as a souvenir of the 'most hideous' exhibition of the century."

While handing me the catalogue, he goes on:

"This reminds me of a very nice Uruguayan painter who came to visit us once at La Californie. He was quite nervous, and after looking at my paintings he couldn't think of anything to say but: 'It's awful. Awful.' No one has ever expressed his admiration in such an odd way."

Suddenly he becomes serious and goes back to the previous subject:

"To tell the truth, even if they had turned half the paintings upside down, what differ-

ence would it have made? Basically it's all the same, isn't it?"

9 January 1967

We are at the old waterfront area in Cannes. Picasso is recovering from hepatitis, which has laid him up for several weeks. Seeing that he is almost well again, the doctors have suggested he get some fresh air.

We stroll to the end of the jetty and watch the boats that are moored a few feet from shore. We talk about regattas, shipwrecks, solitary skippers.

"I had an uncle in Málaga, when I was little, who dreamed of having a boat. He finally managed to buy one very cheap. He dragged it onto land and loaded it with furniture, instruments, beds, stoves, casseroles, compasses, God knows what! A thousand and one things! He stuffed it with so many odds and

At the same restaurant in December 1968. At his right is Aitana Alberti.

ends that when he pushed it back into the water, he could hardly make it out of the port. It went 'pouf' and was swallowed up by the sea."

He does not make it clear whether his uncle was rescued or went down with his ship. But of what importance are such minor details for someone like Picasso? The main point is that it went 'pouf' and was swallowed up by the sea.

Returning along the opposite side of the jetty, we come to a group of small-keeled boats propped on improvised wooden pivots. A sailboat, about fifteen feet long, is sharply outlined against a picture-postcard background. A sailor is painting the hull with an enormous brush. He makes endless brushstrokes in immaculate white. Picasso watches, entranced, from just a few feet away.

"If I didn't see it with my own eyes, I wouldn't believe it," he says. "He's wiping out the landscape."

A little later, as the sun goes down, a brisk breeze pushes us toward the automobile. We drive along slowly in the Croisette area, not knowing exactly where to go—like bored tourists. Suddenly Picasso decides to visit a shop that sells marine paints on the Rue de Batéguier.

When we step out of the car, we notice a large, attractive publicity poster displayed on the facade of the shop. On a vermilion background, capricious yellow letters of various sizes dance about. We take some time absorbing the whole display. It says "Peintures Européenes Sélectionés pour le Yachting. Emails. Vernis. Plastiques."

The proprietor, obviously a bit jittery in the presence of such an unusual client, paces in and out from the back of the shop without quite knowing what to do.

"Show me something unusual," Picasso says. The man returns with a kilo tin of paint under his arm and a tiny bottle. He explains that the paint is always white, and that by just adding a few—or many—drops of the liquid in the little bottle, it is possible to achieve the desired tone of the color chosen. Picasso makes him repeat the instructions several times and selects various colors "in order to try them out": yellow, lilac, blue, and red.

We return to the automobile.

PICASSO: "It's incredible what they invent these days. With this combination of enamel paint and liquid, painting could be revolutionized. Just imagine, an artist can cover the whole canvas white and then, as if his brush were a magic wand, he could paint in the rest with alchemical daubs."

JACQUELINE, teasing affectionately: "You're a real joker, Pablo! Anyone would think this is the first time you ever saw this type of paint!"

## 5 March 1967

PICASSO: "I. have a very strange recurring dream. I dream I'm in London at a hotel near the station. Naturally, it's a neighborhood nobody knows. A neighborhood like so many others, with men, women, children, beggars, girls pounding the pavements. I have a rented studio there and once in a while I go to see if everything is in order. However, I don't paint in it.

"In London I have some acquaintances, such as Bernereggi's father. (Bernereggi was that young Argentine fellow from Barcelona and the Prado, remember?) I think Bernereggi's grandmother is there, too. They're all very fond of me, even pamper me, you know. Ah, yes, someone takes me to a museum, or maybe it's a gallery, to show me what they exhibit there. It's awful stuff."

A good friend of Picasso's is with us during the long monologue. Having been somewhat distracted at the beginning of the conversation, he still does not realize that Picasso is no longer talking about reality, but rather about dreams. When Picasso notices this, he deliberately emphasizes the naturalness of the description:"I also know a neighborhood in Paris no one has ever seen, like the one in London. It's a very peculiar neighborhood, where there are enormous deposits filled with scrap iron. Ghastly. Naturally, I also have a studio there, on the top floor of the tallest building. I go there once in a while to see if everything is in its place, talk with the concierge, who is an impossible person, and then leave."

His friend, judging by a remark he makes a little later, is convinced that Picasso has just taken a new studio in one of the skyscrapers in Montparnasse or some similar place. He only realizes his mistake when he hears the following dream:

"But the worst one that keeps recurring is when I am with Zette Leiris in a popular democracy. I think it's Czechoslovakia. Incredible things happen. The earth trembles, for instance, and Zette Leiris says it isn't so, that I'm wrong. Then I answer her, horrified: 'You're the one who's wrong. Just look at the pavement moving.'"

The friend, a Communist with a sense of humor, guffaws at this. Picasso continues:

"Though, when I think of it, the worst one of them all is a dream I keep having since my operation. I'm flat on a stretcher and a group of doctors is bickering about who's going to operate on me. And I'm stretched out, watching all this, like an object, totally powerless. Awful, isn't it?"

A little while later they discuss whether or not his dreams are in color. Picasso maintains they are, and that the question, which has been put to him a thousand times, is ridiculous:

"What would you dream in if you didn't dream in color? This idiotic idea was undoubtedly invented because of films."

Then the conversation turns to dream and fiction and finally to the curious phenomenon

An animated conversation with a Spanish friend in June 1966.

of the similarity between certain periods of wakefulness and dreams. As we are being called to eat, Picasso hurries to tell one last story related to this subject.

"I had a friend in Barcelona by the name of Planas. He was walking down the Ramblas one day and was suddenly struck dumb when he saw an acquaintance of his approaching. The other fellow, realizing his confusion, couldn't keep from asking:

'What's the matter with you?'

'Nothing. But something very odd just happened. While you were coming toward me, I had the impression you were your brother.'

'But you know I don't have a brother.'

'That's the whole point, and that's why it's so strange.'

From talking about dreams to talking about literature is only a short step. And so, after dinner:

PICASSO: "I remember an amazing story by Alfonso Allais. While having breakfast, a married couple receives a couple of letters. One is for the husband and the other for the wife. The man says to his wife: 'I'll be coming back late tonight. I have to go to a business dinner.' His wife answers: 'That's all right. My mother just wrote asking me to have dinner with her.'

"Actually the letters went like this, more or less: 'Sir, if you would like to see your wife in elegant company, go to the masked ball at such and such an address this evening. She will be dressed as Black Domino,' and 'Madam, if you would like to see your husband in elegant company, go to the masked ball at such and such an address this evening. He will be dressed as Harlequin.'

"Harlequin and Black Domino meet at the ball. When the time to unmask comes, they give each other a hard look. And at this point Allais writes a sensational ending: Neither one is the husband or wife."

Picasso ends his retelling of Allais's story

with a peculiar expression on his face, an expression in which shock and exaltation are mingled:

"It sounds right out of a dream, doesn't it?"

The story of Harlequin and Black Domino is the last of the evening. After bidding us goodnight, Picasso stops at the door of the main room, as if he had forgotten to tell us something important.

"Alfonso Allais's novels," he recalls in a special tone of voice, "were always read to me by Paul Eluard. Only he knew how."

The picture of Eluard remains with us as Picasso climbs the stairs to his room, to dream about London, Paris, an imaginary studio where he never painted, about surgeons and popular democracies. And always in color.

## 12 March 1967

We are again on the subject of dreams and nightmares.

JACQUELINE: "You forgot to tell about that other nightmare you often have. The one about thieves."

PICASSO: "That's true. I've dreamed a lot about thieves lately. I dream that they're robbing me of something. I'm not sure what, but I do know that I wake up screaming 'Stop thief! Stop thief!' Then, on other occasions, I wake up in the night and mull over a thousand things while trying to get back to sleep. It's then I begin to think about not having seen the tiny Degas painting, for instance. The one you saw the other day, remember? Well, at that point I wake Jacqueline and ask her to bring the painting. As soon as I see it, I can begin to think about something else. And sometimes we can't find it. That's frightful. Then I begin to suspect it was carried off by the person I last showed it to in the room I last saw it in. After two months the painting turns up in another place, but meanwhile I'm certain that Kahnweiler, or Pignon, or Maurice Thorez, or even

you stole it. Do you see what I mean about it being frightful? Two months fretting and thinking *that* about a friend!"

However, since he does not like to finish any story on a disagreeable note, he concludes:

"Though, thinking it over, if Kahnweiler had taken it—I end up telling myself in order to calm down—there's no problem. In that case, he has most likely sold it and nothing has been lost."

## 25 August 1967

We are talking about animals. About the owl Picasso had in Antibes in 1947, about the turtles he kept during his days in the Rue des Grands-Augustins, about the goat at La Californie—which actually were two goats according to Hélène Parmelin's version—but mainly we talk about monkeys.

Picasso tells a couple of amusing stories. A long time ago, when he was living on the Rue de la Boëtie in Paris, someone gave him a monkey. It destroyed so much in the apartment that he had to dispose of it.

"I finally asked Sabartès to give it away, and he managed to find some gypsies to take it off. A few weeks later he saw the monkey performing in the street with his new masters, more docile than a circus horse. No doubt they accomplished that miracle with a good strong stick."

The second story is more impressive:

PICASSO: "I don't know how it came about, but I went to the zoological gardens in Paris once. They had a monkey there which really flabbergasted me with its intelligence, and I returned a number of times to see it. You probably won't believe this, but it's true. One day, after many visits—by this time the monkey and I were on very friendly terms—I noticed it scouring the ground for something. It finally turned up with a piece of glass."

He is totally absorbed in the story of the

On an outing. When this photo was taken, Picasso was singing an old Spanish folksong.

monkey. He rises from his white armchair, and from then on illustrates the story with histrionic gestures:

PICASSO: "I see the monkey approach the wall at the back of the cage and begin to scribble on it."

Picasso looks for a patch of empty wall space and, like an accomplished actor, mimes the animal's scribbling performance. Then he backs away from the wall, crosses his arms, and contemplates the results of the imaginary drawing. Then he starts drawing again and contemplates "the masterpiece." The drama is repeated several times. He concludes:

"Fantastic, really. It suddenly struck me, like a thunderbolt, that between the monkey and Michelangelo or the monkey and me, there is basically very little difference."

12 September 1967

Six in the afternoon. We are having tea at a pastry shop on the Rue d'Antibes. The wallpaper is a lush rose-vine pattern that looks more like a jungle. It is black and gray on a cream-colored background. From a distance the tables seem to be marble, but when we sit down we discover they are actually plastic. The red-and-black chairs vaguely suggest a certain English style. The waitresses wear starched white aprons and collars. We are surrounded by aged ladies, all picturesquely and uniformly attired: pearl beads, leather caps, and lavish quantities of rings and bracelets.

"It's frightening," says Picasso, "like a wax museum."

After tea we drive through the streets of Cannes. The conversation is pleasant and light-hearted.

Though we are following no definite route, we are heading toward Golfe Juan, with Picasso in the front seat. Now we can make out the illuminated silhouette of an Italian transat-

Picasso explains that this plaster copy of a Michelangelo *Slave* and the one on the opposite page lay forgotten in the basement of the Antibes Museum long before it was called the Picasso Museum. "They let me take them home, but I had to give them a heap of my work in exchange."

lantic liner from the highway. It is the *Michelangelo*, sister ship, if I am not mistaken, to the *Leonardo da Vinci* and the *Raffaello*.

"It's a good idea," someone says, "to name ships after painters. Someday there will probably be a battleship named Gutiérrez Solana and a destroyer named Pablo Picasso."

Picasso picks up the mention of his friend Solana:

"Solana was marvelous," he recollects. "When he first came to Paris, he took a taxi at the Gare d'Orléans and told the driver, just as if he were in a small Castilian town: 'To the *fonda*' [the local inn]. As if *fondas* were universal civic amenities. After a few days he came to see me at home and I asked him what impression he had of Paris. He answered, quite seriously: 'It reminds me of Rif.'"

After a short pause Picasso continues:

"He said it in such a serious, formal way. Solana was scarcely the man to carry on a humorous conversation, like us. And maybe he

was right. Who knows? Perhaps Paris is more like Rif than, say, Shanghai or the Philippines."

He ends in his characteristic manner, almost as if talking to himself:

"We all know why we say certain things. Or see certain things."

Then he turns completely around to face the back seat of the car. He had been totally absorbed in his monologue, but now he wants to contemplate the effect on his audience.

"On the other hand, Solana, for example, couldn't understand some subtleties on quite serious matters. On one occasion Eugenio D'Ors visited his studio to look at his work. The only comment he made before leaving was that Solana's style was very 'Egyptian.' An amazing coincidence! It was just what Douanier Rousseau once said about me, contrasting his work and mine: that he was a modern painter, while I was a young painter with an Egyptian style. Well, Manolo Solana told me the story about Eugenio D'Ors and added: 'Can you imagine

that, Pablo? An Egyptian style! He must be an imbecile. I don't know how I stood it and why I didn't hit him.'"

Picasso cannot let the moral of the story go unstated:

"Now, in this case D'Ors, who was really a fool, was absolutely right. Or at least he knew what he wanted to say, as Douanier did when he said I was an Egyptian-style painter."

8 January 1968

"How are the musketeers, Pablo?"
"They're finished."
"And the nudes?"
"They're finished, too. I'm only doing lancers now. Bengal lancers." He explains that a few days before, he had seen the old film *The Bengal Lancers* on television, and that it had kept going through his head. Picasso rarely watches television, but every rule has its exception, and a short time ago he went through a period in which he did not miss a single wrestling match.

To get back to Picasso's lancers, the same phenomenon as that of the 1962 warriors or the 1957 Meñinas or the 1967 musketeers is occurring. Once embarked on a special subject, he cannot abandon it. It is as if he were the victim of a fatal obsession. But his whole artistic life is the history of an obsession, a restless, explosive search that has been going on for three-quarters of a century.

He shows me the drawings. "There's still no painting to boast about on the lancers theme." The truth of the matter is that I can see no connection whatever between the famous adventure film and what he has done in four or five days of frenetic activity. At first glance, they strike me as variations on the painter and model theme. A bearded sultan, fully dressed, impassive, always shown in profile, confronts one, two, or three odalisques who are nude to the waist. Enormous breasts. Tracings that hint at a misty Oriental decoration.

"It seems more like a harem," I comment.

He does not hear me. He talks in a loud voice unusual for him, as if he were conversing with himself.

"I don't know what's happening to me lately. I do nothing but lancers, musketeers, warriors, bullfighters."

"True enough. It's your obsession for the lance, sword, and rapier. You'll have to see a psychoanalyst."

"You're joking, but it's true. Not about the psychoanalyst, of course. But it's all related. Everything has a hidden meaning. For example, why did you put on a blue shirt today exactly the same color as the one I'm wearing? Don't you see? The world is full of odd things."

In one of the drawings the sultan is carrying a flower in his hand instead of the scepter he flashes in others.

PICASSO: "Look, look here! In this drawing the lance has turned into a flower. How strange!"

As far as I can see, there are no signs of lances anywhere.


20 May 1968

Picasso is showing a handful of engravings done during April and May. There are large ones and small ones, splattered with the most far-fetched characters: saltimbanques, musketeers, Moors from Rif—according to Picasso's description—and women, children, and old men.

As usually happens, one engraving in particular attracts our attention and we linger over it, studying it longer than we have the previous ones. Alert as ever to the smallest detail, Picasso comes over to us and laughs, a roguish look in his eye as he puts his index finger on a character at the lower edge of the picture:

"You see, that's La Celestina. She has fallen on the floor and lost her money. Do you see those scrawls here?"

There is a brief pause while I look at some delicate strokes that coil one atop another, like confetti, or a cobweb.

"Well, those are the coins she's lost." [La Celestina is the heroine—both bawd and procuress—of Fernando de Rojas's late-fifteenth-century classic of the same name.]

Seeing that I am amazed by his explanation of the drawing, Picasso continues enthusiastically:

"Of course, one never knows what's going to come out, but as soon as the drawing gets underway, a story or an idea is born. And that's it. Then the story grows, like theater or life—and the drawing is turned into other drawings, a real novel. It's great fun, believe me. At least, I enjoy myself no end inventing these stories, and I spend hour after hour while I draw, observing my creatures and thinking about the mad things they're up to. Basically, it's my way of writing fiction."

Then he goes on to show us a series of engravings, each only slightly different from the next

"Yes, yes. You see, they are different 'stages' of the same story. Sometimes I correct, other times not. Look at this one: there's a number next to the date, in Roman numerals. What number is it? Six? Well, I made six different engravings that day on the same little story—or maybe more."

Now Picasso is showing us the next engraving, though he seems distracted. It looks like a woman, surrounded by saltimbanques, swimming in a transparent aquarium.

"I did this thinking about André Breton's mistress. She used to swim in a circus."

I wait for a logical continuation of the story, but Picasso puts the engraving down on a chair, crosses his arms, and goes back to our previous conversation:

Picasso listens attentively to the Chicago architect William Hartmann.

"You know, I've always thought that if I could continue the same drawing, the same story, to the very end, the last possible limits—do you know what I mean? Well, if that happened, I think the painting, or drawing, would finally talk to you."

We have been looking at engravings for half an hour and there is still another folder we have not yet seen.

I: "But what an incredible number of drawings you've done in a month and a half! How many are there, more or less?"

JACQUELINE: "Two hundred."

I: "Two hundred? That can't possibly be."

PICASSO, satisfied: "Yes, probably there are two hundred. Who cares? The main thing is to pass the time of day, isn't it?"

22 May 1968

Six in the afternoon. Jacqueline turns on the television set after tea. Her action is most unusual at Notre Dame de Vie, but the events transpiring in France these last weeks make us all avid for news. Like so many other millions of spectators at this moment, we are gathering to listen to a live broadcast of the vote of confidence from the National Assembly, which should take place any minute. Will De Gaulle's government fall? At first glance it seems that the whole matter leaves Picasso cold, but that does not prevent him from following the debate with great interest, in his inimitable way. While the first speakers talk, he makes one joke after another about their attitudes and gestures, their ability to command words.

"The secret," he says, "seems to consist in quoting great writers, and, above all, great poets. Yesterday a deputy quoted Kafka, another one quoted Cocteau, and then someone else quoted Apollinaire."

He has no sooner finished saying this when a speaker quotes Charles Péguy. We burst into

In the main room at Notre Dame de Vie.

laughter and become almost delirious when somebody else quotes Goethe. As if that were not enough, the speaker then synopsizes a scene from Shaw's *Pygmalion*.

Picasso recognizes his old friend André Malraux, seated with the other ministers next to Georges Pompidou. The author of *Man's Fate* has a worried look on his face, in keeping with the circumstances. He rests his head between his hands for a long moment.

"Poor Malraux! He looks distraught," Picasso observes compassionately.

After an hour, the President of the Assembly announces the voting results:

"There are 244 votes in favor of the motion to censure, 233 against," and Picasso whips back:

"It is not finished. It's only just beginning." This is much the same thing the students on the streets of Paris will be shouting this very evening: "This is not the conclusion, the battle continues."

3 June 1968

We are alone in the main room of Notre Dame de Vie. As on so many other occasions, we are talking about the Surrealists. Picasso reminds himself of a book he promised to show me a few days ago. It is the original manuscript of *Le Con d'Hellène*, an erotic book attributed to Louis Aragon by bibliophiles and Aragon's friends. There are some very daring pictures of a certain notorious lady known by the name of Kiki de Montparnasse. He returns in a few minutes.

"I couldn't find it. I'll look for it and show it to you another time. But I did come across *L'Immaculée Conception*."

He shows it to me. As he had told me before, the original manuscript is covered with corrections written in by the two authors, Paul Eluard and André Breton.

"Just look at this automatic poetry. This poetry is as automatic as I am an Egyptian-style

Jacqueline with her postcard collection of Picasso reproductions.

painter, as Rousseau used to say. But maybe Rousseau was right; certainly I am more of an Egyptian in my painting than Breton and Eluard are automatic poets."

Then, quite unexpectedly, he begins to talk about Françoise Gilot's book. It is a theme he finds repugnant, and he avoids it whenever the book is mentioned. If he is asked about it, he immediately changes the subject. Today, however, he is the one to bring it up, probably because of the photos of Kiki de Montparnasse.

"What I can't understand," he says, "is why they didn't publish that book, Françoise's, with pictures of me in the buff, like Kiki. Though, of course, they would have been a little difficult to come by."

"Don't you know, Pablo, they do wonders with photography? They could have made a photomontage combining your face and some pornographic photos."

"Of course! I don't know why the devil they didn't think of that. People really aren't very imaginative. They would have made a lot more money by now if they *had* done it that way. Have you read the book?"

"Yes."

"What did you think of it?"

"Bad. But you don't come out in as unfavorable a light as you think. Just 50 percent is unfavorable."

"Well, I've been told otherwise. And some paragraphs have been read to me. The part that makes me laugh is when she has me pontificating about Michelangelo, Van Gogh, Velázquez, and God knows who! As if I were an art critic! Did I say an art critic! As if I were a professor at the Royal Academy of San Fernando!"

He is referring ironically to his usual manner of speaking, which is at the opposite pole from an academic's Cartesian discourse. It is a style well known to his intimates, and is based on paradox, contradiction, and synthesis. It is, in my opinion, the mental mechanism of an intuitive, dialectical nature.

"Besides, as everybody knows, I detest talking seriously about painting. And even more, I detest talking seriously about anything at all. It's the best way for people not to understand each other. Don't you think so?"

As I agree with him, I think that this friend of mine, Picasso, is an incredible character—in short, a real rebel. There is not the slightest doubt that the so-called "intellectual"—whether he is an art critic or an art historian—has always passed the same judgment on Picasso that today's young rebels pass on the academic discourses delivered by the majority of their professors.

"What I can't fathom is why they're forever making me say improbable things. If I were a taciturn, silent type like Miró, for instance, then I could understand why they'd have to invent conversation. But I'm not. I'm forever jabbering. I remember once a critic reading aloud the first sentence of a book he was doing on me. It went like this, more or less: 'Picasso confessed to me not long ago that the shortest distance between two points was a straight line.' Can you imagine? Naturally, I didn't let him read any further, but said; 'Listen here. Are you sure I discovered that?'"

And, after a pause:

"I also thought that if I had been the Greek who invented that law, I would most certainly have stated it differently."

Well, maybe yes, maybe no. But that does not matter, as Picasso himself says about almost anything. What does matter is what he is trying to say when he says what he says. And my experience is that if one knows how to listen to him, one sees that his reasoning is as sharp as that of Cervantes. So I say:

"Pablo, the problem is one of 'communication,' as they say nowadays. One has to have the 'key.' Not only to understand you, but every other human being. Even if it happens to be more complicated in your case than it is with other people."

"Of course, that's it. The problem is the 'key.' Eluard, for example, had the key. In fact, he had all the keys."

While I write down these lines a few hours later, I go on talking with him mentally:

"Well, yes and no, like everything else. There were many, Pablo, who had the key, even if you don't remember it just now. Max Jacob, Apollinaire, Gertrude Stein, Paul Eluard, Satie, André Salmon, the false Baron Mollet, Fernande Olivier, Soto, Eva, Pallarés, Tristan Tzara, Sabartès, Ilya Ehrenburg, Manolo, Rafaël Alberti, Enrique Arias, Manolo Angeles Ortiz, Jacqueline—perhaps the 'key' is shared among them. If there is one, of course. If there is one."

### 25 August 1968

The publisher and bibliophile Louis Broder has just arrived from Paris to show Picasso the proofs of Max Jacob's *Testament*. A limited edition is about to appear. Jacob wrote it in 1944, while he was imprisoned by the Gestapo in the concentration camp at Drancy, but it has never been published. Picasso has made this meticulous edition possible by contributing some choice engravings from his recent work, and is happy to see his name together with Jacob's once more. Last year he made feasible another great French poet's posthumous text, *Sables Mouvent* by Pierre Reverdy, which Broder also published. Reverdy and Picasso were close friends for many years, and we had watched Picasso dedicate one of the first copies—with a magnificent drawing, a strange feminine profile—about a year ago.

Broder has also brought the original manuscript of Jacob's *Testament* with him. He shows it to us and we can see how pleased and moved he is by it. The beginning of the text is written

Picasso shows a drawing he finished just recently, on 5 August, 1967, for *Sable Mouvents*, written by his friend Pierre Reverdy and published posthumously by the Paris publisher Louis Broder.

in the most delicate calligraphy, and is made even more poignant by our recollection of the ghastly circumstances of Jacob's life in 1944 and the fate that awaited him:

"I bequeath all my good to those who consider it such. I bequeath all my bad to those who consider it good."

Going over the manuscript, we notice a series of pen drawings superimposed on the text in Jacob's hand. they have nothing to do with the words. It is as if the poet had two distinct ideas simultaneously while he wrote the text. Or as if the drawings had been done on another day altogether. There are recumbent female figures and complicated male profiles sketched alongside and right over the text.

Picasso is deeply moved by the sight of the manuscript. As usually happens when conversation turns to some long-gone friend, however, he seems to want to evoke only joyous memories.

PICASSO: "When he was converted to Catholicism, they baptized him in a convent on the Rue d'Assas, if I'm not mistaken, and I was his godfather. Just imagine, a godfather at a baptism! Then the ridiculous scene when we all waited around at the convent for something to drink—perhaps because it was an important conversion. Or at least I thought it was. But they gave us nothing, and we had to move off to a café to celebrate.

"I wanted them to give him the baptismal name of Fiacre, because there is a St. Fiacre. The patron saint of gardeners, I think, but it wasn't possible. He finally chose Cyprian himself. I don't know why."

Someone recalls Jacob's trip to Spain and an excursion to Toledo with the writer José Bergamín. At the portal of the Toledo cathedral Jacob apparently fell into a trance, went down on his knees, and began to insist the devil was there.

PICASSO: "Yes, yes. The devil often appeared

A view of the sculpture room.

to Max. But most incredible is that he had become a great believer and wanted to fulfill his religious duties rigorously—fasting, Lent, everything. He came to my house on a Friday and, when he saw there was a stew with sausage for supper, he asked, somewhat alarmed:

'Is the sausage meatless?'

'Oh yes, it's meatless,' I answered.

He trusted me, and ate the stew without a moment's hesitation."

### 27 November 1968

Today Picasso greets us surrounded by shirts. There are shirts on the sofa, shirts on the chairs, shirts on the floor, shirts draped over a gigantic package of pencils, and shirts on the layout of a book that is in preparation. Someone has discovered Picasso's weakness for shirts, and the word has spread around the world. Now Picasso receives them by the dozen as gifts from all sorts of places.

"These are from Barcelona," he says, displaying a pile of shirts in various colors.

While we are looking them over, he recalls the time Harry Truman came to La Californie and showed more interest in his shirts than in his paintings.

"Of course," he concludes gleefully, "it was then I discovered he had been a haberdasher before he became president."

We continue to examine the shirts one by one, as if they were a series of drawings, when Charles Feld, director of the publishing company Editions Cercle d'Art, comes in. He is carrying a bulky package under his arm, and for a brief moment it crosses our minds that he is also bringing a few dozen shirts. Luckily, we are mistaken. He is carrying the layout of a future book, so we discreetly take our leave in order to let them work.

Picasso's work table in the sculpture room.

When we return, Picasso and Feld have had time to talk and have begun to leaf through the future book. Picasso turns back the pages he has just seen and shows us the title: *Picasso, Drawings 1966–1968.* Then he asks Feld:

"How many drawings are there in all?"

"Four hundred."

"Four hundred? Not bad, is it? I hope the people who take the trouble to look at them will find them more interesting than what they read in the newspapers."

Picasso continues leafing through the opening pages of the layout, totally absorbed. They contain truly magnificent reproductions of his latest drawings, and strike us as one more proof that the master is still surpassing himself, prodigally creating masterpieces without any diminution caused by age, or time, or the fact that he has already attempted just about everything as far as drawing is concerned, during the course of his long life. Musketeers, bawds, Bengal lancers, nudes, portraits of tall people, short people, young people, old people, bearded gentlemen and clean-shaven gentlemen, more musketeers, more nudes parade before our eyes. Suddenly, turning a page, a series of particularly curious Bengal lancers takes our fancy. There are ten or twenty drawings on the same theme: a group of nude young women, who seem to be part of an enviable harem, in various postures of bathers in repose. And, in the middle, there is always a pool with a solitary female swimmer.

"I've never seen an indoor pool but I imagine it must be like this. Well, actually I could have copied Ingres, but I realized it wasn't worth the bother. Certainly Ingres didn't see an enclosed pool in his life and simply invented them for his paintings. Anyway, there weren't pools in his time."

After we have looked at them, Picasso puts the loose octavo folders that make up the

Lunching under the pergola at Notre Dame de Vie with Jacqueline's daughter, Cathy.

layout to one side and gathers them together on the table. He continues to turn the pages gently with his alchemist's hands—those small hands that someone commented on only yesterday, much to his pleasure. But his attention suddenly focuses on a page on which four portraits reproduced in full color stand out, fabulously inventive and utterly enchanting.

PICASSO: "*Caramba!* I'd forgotten these completely."

FELD: "You see? A book like this is basically useful. At least it is for you. It even helps you recall your own drawings."

PICASSO: "But—I didn't remember this drawing either, or that one. It's amazing what you can forget."

What is really amazing is that he can remember 394 drawings perfectly and has forgotten only six. Especially when we realize that in this short period he has also made 500

engravings and heaven knows how many other paintings.

But he is already looking at something else, superbly erotic drawings of a kissing couple on the verge of consuming one another.

PICASSO: "And won't you have any problems with censorship?"

FELD: "And won't you have any problems with censorship?"

FELD: "You know, Louise Leiris is about to exhibit my latest engravings. And there's one series that is quite innocent—I mean, quite natural. Well, you can imagine what they are about: Raphael and La Fornarina—his famous model—making love. Well, there's no need to exaggerate—it's not all sex, Raphael is painting in many of them, too—but Michelangelo is also there, spying on them from behind the draperies or under the bed. And sometimes the Pope is peeping through the keyhole, or some other important character is lurking

178

Lunching indoors.

about. Anyway, they have to do with certain facts—I would call them historical facts. And do you know what they've told Madame Leiris? They've told her she will not be able to publish a catalogue, that it can't be bound. She'll have to publish loose pages, without sewing them together!"

Feld explains that there are laws in France prohibiting certain types of publications, but he doesn't think they apply to his book of Picasso drawings.

PICASSO: "On the other hand, isn't it the fashionable thing to teach these things to schoolchildren nowadays? Aren't they talking about sex education everywhere? Believe me, I am a master in this field. Take my word for it."

We all laugh uproariously at this declaration, but Picasso's tone and manner remain theatrically serious.

PICASSO: "Instead of carrying on this foolishness with me, they'd be better off publishing a textbook for schoolchildren with this catalogue. Don't you agree?"

28 November 1968

PICASSO: "I'm beginning to be considered a famous author. Do you know that? Gustavo Gili is going to publish *The Burial of the Count of Orgaz* in Barcelona, and Gallimard is going to bring out another play of mine very soon. A play you don't know, written in French. I'll show it to you. The title? *Les Quatre Petites Filles* [The Four Little Girls].

I tell him that I've heard the title, as *Las Cuatros Doncellitas en el Jardín* [The Four Little Maidens in the Garden], cited by one of the many Picasso scholars. Though now I realize the text could not have been known to anyone, since it has not yet been published.

PICASSO: "*Doncellas*, maidens, no. No, no. *Niñas*, girls, yes. That I'm sure of, but I'm not

At a restaurant in Cannes with a group of Spanish friends. At Picasso's left is the author's mother.

sure of the garden. I suppose I wrote 'vegetable garden' and then crossed it out. It's all the same."

He goes on to tell me that he has another unpublished piece for the theater, *The Bullfight in Mourning*, written "long before *The Burial of the Count* and *The Four Little Girls.*"

PICASSO: "It's more than forty pages, according to what Miguel told me. He's typing it up. [Miguel Mariano is Picasso's secretary, who had come back to work with Picasso in 1968, after twenty years' absence. He had also worked as his secretary in Paris during the 1940s.] It's really funny to think I've managed to write so many pages on the bullfight but still haven't led my first bull into the ring. Forty pages and I still haven't been able to begin the bullfight!"

With childlike enthusiasm tinged with the subtlest of self-criticism he adds:

"But it is very funny. They take me seriously, as if I were a genuine author. Just think,

Gallimard is even talking about author's rights and all that! What if everyone ends up thinking I'm a serious writer?"

After a brief silence, feigning the most ponderous tone, he says:

"At heart I feel I am a poet who has gone astray. Don't you agree?"

Naturally I tell him yes, but I cannot keep from immediately qualifying his last remark.

"But you haven't gone so far astray."

4 December 1968

The first copies of *The Four Little Girls* have arrived. Picasso is overjoyed. He tells us somewhat later that this play has had "a long life, and because of that, a stormy one." He wrote it in 1947, with no thought of publishing it, but some years later yielded to a publisher's request and sent the manuscript to Paris. However, unsure of himself like any other novice poet, he changed his mind that same

With Francisco Bores, a Spanish painter of the so-called School of Paris.

night and telephoned the next day demanding the manuscript be returned.

PICASSO: "Gallimard didn't even have time to read it, because my order to return the text arrived before the manuscript."

He signs three copies for us, writing the most uninhibited dedications imaginable with the greatest of ease. They are composed in pure Navas de Malvivir style, and there is a great laugh every time he signs "the author."

"Don't laugh," I finally say, after half an hour of listening to his amusing self-disparagement. "It might just happen you'll be considered a better poet than painter at some future date. What would you say if a dictionary published in the year 3000 spoke about you like this: 'Pablo Picasso, great Andalusian poet, better known in his lifetime as a painter'?"

He has stopped smiling and has become very serious before I finish my last sentence.

"Very strange," he says. "What you're saying right now is the same thing a young boy once told me. That boy became very famous in Spain later—what was his name—the son of the dictator—the one who founded the Falange?"

"José Antonio Primo de Rivera?"

"Yes, that's it. Primo de Rivera. He said exactly the same thing you said a minute ago. Exactly. At a banquet in my honor at the San Sebastián Yacht Club. Strange, isn't it?"

And what started as a gentle autumn evening, more or less literary, is unexpectedly transformed into an evocation of the preliminaries to the Spanish Civil War.

"José Antonio was quite charming," Picasso says later. "On the other hand, the journalist who accompanied him was far less so. Just listen to what he said about my eyes, or rather the look in them. That I had the same expression as Mussolini. Of course, that was a compliment of sorts, coming from him. However, for me it was anything but. I knew the people wining and dining me that night were

The Norwegian sculptor Nesjar shows photographs for his Marseilles sculpture project.

very dangerous, and as I remember I boarded the train for France that same evening. And that was my last day in Spain."

19 December 1968

Pilar, who was Sabartès's combination secretary and chief-of-staff during his last years, has just arrived. Picasso greets her with affection and asks how everything is in Barcelona. He tells us later, in his usual lighthearted tone but not entirely without an overtone of sadness:

"What a brute I am! I was about to ask after Sabartès."

He reveals that he still dedicates engravings to the dead Sabartès, just as if he were alive, "with the date and everything." His voice becomes endlessly tender when he says:

"The only things I don't write into the dedications are my outrageous remarks—like before."

Pilar says that Sabartès left a series of Picasso drawings and voluminous correspondence in a package, with strict orders that it not be opened for fifty years.

PICASSO, who can scarcely believe his ears: "How many years?"

PILAR: "Fifty."

PICASSO: "Fifty years! Wasn't that a bit far-fetched of him? And what's in the package?"

PILAR, almost offended: "Well, I don't know, Don Pablo. I didn't even want to look. Any wish or order of Don Jaime's is sacred to me. Besides, the more I think about him the more I realize what a superior person he was, a man who was right about everything. And I think if he decided to have it that way, there must have been very good reasons."

Picasso's prolonged silence is the most eloquent answer to this flood of affection and respect for his recently deceased friend.

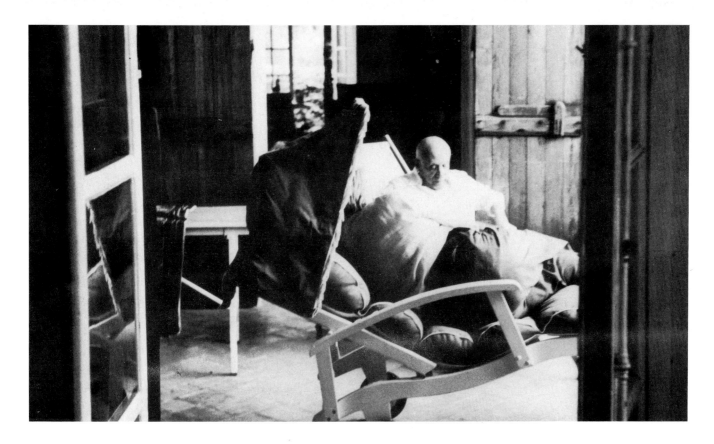

On the small terrace off the bedroom.

However, his eyes sparkle with the immense curiosity she has aroused with the mere mention of this mysterious package.

"I'll have to see about this Sabartès," he says finally, talking as if Sabartès were alive. "He always thought I could do anything. Undoubtedly he thinks he'll force me to live another fifty years because of this secret bundle."

18 January 1969

Conversation turns to *The Four Little Girls, The Burial of the Count of Orgaz,* and *The Bullfight in Mourning.* Picasso leaves the room and comes back with an unpublished poem of his engraved in metal. He also shows us an artist's proof of the engraving.

PICASSO: "You can't imagine the trouble it took to do this. I had to draw in each letter backwards. Naturally, it's easy to get mixed up. For instance, here it says CONDOM. I probably wanted to write CORDON, but this is how it came out and that's how I'm leaving it."

A few minutes later our conversation turns to poetic style, the magic of words, and the inimitable characteristic voice natural to any great poet at any time in history.

PICASSO: "The same is true of painting. For example, I had a good friend, a hundred years ago or so, called Padilla. Well, Padilla was a painter and had given me a gift of one of his paintings, a landscape, which was really pretty awful. I've thought about this landscape over and over—don't ask me why this particular landscape—but I always have the same thought, that if Cézanne had done it in exactly the same way—you know what I mean, using the same colors in the same way—well, it would have been completely different.

"And I've always thought that if Michelangelo had said, one fine day: 'Today I am going to paint like Raphael,' then the painting, which

183

he could have done imitating Raphael down to the last detail, would still have been a Michelangelo. And if Raphael had wanted to imitate Michelangelo—what am I saying? copy Michelangelo—it would have come out a Raphael anyway."

After a pause, he opens his eyes wide and leans close to the person next to him, as if to emphasize the confidential tone of the conversation:

"With writers much the same happens. Many years ago a friend of mine, who wrote for the magazine *Blanco y Negro*, promised to write a special text for one of the issues of *Arte Joven*. The day came when we asked for the article. He had to be coaxed a good bit, but finally he pulled out some pages. Do you know what he read to us? Nothing less than the beginning of *Don Quixote!* However, read by him, Cervantes was not the same: it was a mess. On the other hand, the exact opposite occurred when Paul Eluard read something. He would often read the newspaper to me and something extraordinary would take place: the newspaper turned into a fabulous literary text and I could listen by the hour, dumbfounded."

Picasso glances questioningly at each of the friends surrounding him, as if to measure the effect of his words. Then he sips some tea and concludes, like an oracle:

"And the same thing happens with the bulls. A good bull is born and so is a bad one. And every good bull is different from the one before. Even among those from the same ranch, where they all bear the same lineage and have been raised in the same way. There are simply brave bulls and less brave bulls. You can think what you like about this, but that's how it is."

## February 1969

I bring him the gift of a book today. It is the French edition of John Berger's *The Success and Failure of Picasso*. Its working hypothesis is impressive, and so are its bold conclusions, some of which are quite critical so far as Picasso's recent work is concerned. I'm interested in drawing Picasso out on one of the book's theses, the one touching on Picasso's artistic frustration beginning in 1944, which stemmed from the Communist Party's lack of comprehension about his work. "In becoming a communist, Picasso hoped to come out of his exile," Berger says. "In fact the communists treated him as everybody else had done. That is to say, they separated the man from his work. They honoured the former and equivocated about the latter."

Three days later I ask him if he has read the book. He says he has glanced at it before going to sleep. His comments are, as usual, only half serious.

"He must be a pretty bad painter, because he writes fairly well. He doesn't make as many blunders as most of the others who have written about me."

I ask him what he thinks about the passage dealing with the Communist Party and his painting. He hasn't read it, he says, and I realize the roles have been reversed. Now it is he who is trying to draw me out. At his request, I summarize the essential facts for him.

PICASSO: "Perhaps he's right, perhaps not, like everything. Although, thinking it over, maybe he really is right. Because, what I accomplished in painting was truly Socialist Realism, and 'they' simply didn't realize it."

## 14 February 1969

We are dining in Antibes with Christian and Yvonne Zervos. The publisher of the famous Picasso catalogue has had 295 of the master's recent paintings photographed today, and he is satisfied with his work.

ZERVOS: "There are periods when it is very difficult to do anything with him, as you know,

Jacqueline with Kaboul, Picasso's last Afghan hound.

periods when he doesn't want to see anybody. This isn't the first time I've had to spend a long time waiting in Cannes to see him. But years ago it was different, and sometimes he even accompanied me to pick up paintings I needed to photograph—paintings he didn't have at home. I remember once—it must have been in 1934 or 1935—we went to the Bank of France, where he stored a number of canvases in a room rented in the basement. Well, we chose the paintings and set them aside to pick up another day, when they'd be carefully packed. The bank guards closed the door after us and then Picasso said to me, winking his eye like a mischievous schoolboy: 'I have two more rooms. Do you want to see them?' I said I did, of course, and he had another armored room opened for us."

Zervos, well aware of the interest he has kindled in us, pauses while he carefully consumes a delectable sea urchin and savors his white wine. He continues:

"Haven't I ever told you this story? Wait till you see what happens. You'll see. Well, the second room was even bigger than the first, almost as big as this restaurant. To my amazement, there were no paintings in it, but only packages, piled one atop the other to the height, say, of Picasso. Between these piles of packages there was a kind of labyrinthine trench that enabled one to reach the packages piled against the walls. I thought they were drawings, or engravings, or letters—perhaps the Apollinaire archives—in short, something on that order."

Another pause to eat another couple of sea urchins and to drink a few more glasses of wine. The very least one can say about Zervos is that this fastidious notary of Picasso's work is also a genuine master of suspense.

ZERVOS: "Well, as I was saying, Picasso goes up to one of the packages like a mischievous child, tears the paper off one of the corners, and shows me what's inside. And do you know

Picasso in January 1969 with Frederic Dürbach, who created tapestries based on
Picasso's designs.

what there was inside? *Bank Notes!* Yes, sir,
bank notes, the largest denomination that
existed in France then, which was enormous."

The theme and variations on "Picasso and
Money" have been wildly fantasized in books
and magazines the world over, but I had never
read nor imagined a tale like this.

ZERVOS: "As you see, instead of depositing
his money in a bank account and earning
interest, as any other person in his position
would have done, he preferred having it in
bundles, wrapped in newspaper. He's always
been a bit of a peasant about many things, not
only this. He's really no different from the
country bumpkin who keeps his savings sewn
into his mattress."

A few days later I ask Picasso if what Zervos
told us is true. He answers in the affirmative,
not giving the matter the slightest importance.

"How awful!" I say, exaggerating a bit in the
hope of making him talk. "You must have lost

a bit here and there, what with inflation and
the post-war devaluation."

"You're wrong. Not so. I haven't lost one
cent."

And he tells me this marvelous story about
Jorge Bomberg:

PICASSO: "I had a friend in Paris during my
Rue de la Boëtie days who was Argentinian,
the son of bankers or something like that. He
had never done a lick of work in his life. In
those days, Argentinians were very fashionable
in Paris, and people fought to have one or two
as permanent guests at their gatherings. The
ideal Argentinian could sing tangos and dance
like a ballroom professional. Of course, those
ideal Argentinians weren't all that easy to come
by. My Argentinian could neither sing nor
dance, but he had another rare virtue. He was
the best Picasso counterfeiter who ever existed."

Picasso sips his "Queen of the Fields" tea and

With Frederic Dürbach the younger.

I recall those moments of suspense with Zervos at the restaurant in Antibes. I savor every moment, thinking that if this story of Picasso's money becomes much more rococo it will turn into the thousand and second Arabian Night.

PICASSO: "As I was saying, this fellow Bomberg was a sensational forger. He would come to see me at my studio, take a quick look at my latest painting, and ask me if I had finished it yet. Then he would invite me to his house a few days later for a meal. When we'd go into the dining room, the same scene would be enacted every time. The first thing to swim into sight would be *My Painting* hanging on the wall. Can you imagine? What a memory! And the copy was perfect! Just as well he was as rich as Croesus and never sold any. He painted them as a joke on me, all in fun."

"And what happened to him?"

"He died some years ago in Switzerland. In a madhouse, I think."

"And what happened to the paintings?"

"Well, I don't know. Good heavens, you're right! Probably they're in circulation. In museums. Good heavens!"

The thought of this eventuality makes Picasso burst into laughter, but I don't want to lose track of our original conversation.

"What I can't understand is Bomberg's connection to your bank notes."

"Well, one day he wrote me saying I should send my money to Switzerland because it was going to be worthless in France. And I sent it to Switzerland because I trusted him. And that's how I saved it."

It seems we have reached the end of the story with this bank transfer which he owed to the advice of his most dedicated forger. But Picasso goes on: "Of course, I never saw the money again. They invested it there; then the war came along and I forgot about it. Occasionally, a banker comes to see me and

With a group of Spanish friends.

says: 'There are no longer so-and-so-many thousand pesetas but so-and-so-many something elses.' Always a little more, according to the bank man. But I haven't seen it since. Actually, I think it would have been better if I had left it as it was, don't you?"

Some guests are announced, and he only has time for one last remark:

"Anyway, it's all the same. What the devil difference is the money to me? My life is my work!"

## 17 February 1969

Zervos complains today that his work with Picasso is going very slowly. There are still "at least 10,000 things to catalogue," and when he comes to Cannes, he never knows whether he'll be able to photograph the works or not.

Then he forgets his main concern for a moment and nostalgically recounts how he came to "dedicate" himself to Picasso.

ZERVOS: "I published the first catalogue in 1932, but I published the first reproductions in 1924. Forty-five years ago."

He recollects his days as a student of Philosophy and Letters at the Sorbonne, where he did his thesis on medieval and Byzantine art. Wandering around Paris one day, mulling over his thesis material, he chanced to walk by Vollard's shop. There was a Matisse show on and some of the paintings of the now-celebrated French master were on display in the window. Zervos was suddenly struck by the similarity between a certain period in Byzantine painting and the work on exhibit. Just at that moment Vollard looked out and said: "Are you interested, young man? Well, come in. There are many more inside by the same painter." Zervos went in and discovered not only Matisse's work but also Picasso's, for Vollard had some of those as well.

ZERVOS: "That is how, on a winter afternoon, I came to choose my Road to Damascus. Do

From left to right: Manolo Angeles Ortíz, Francisco Bores, and Rafaël Alberti.
Picasso wears a gift brought from Italy which is ingeniously fashioned to
represent a pair of breasts.

you realize—forty-five years publishing this man's work!"

When I repeat the anecdote to Picasso, he feigns anger:

"His Road to Damascus! Can you imagine? And what about me? Or do you think it's fun to have to stop work to find my blue paintings or Egyptian-period canvases to show Zervos? Or to tell him on what date I did such-and-such a drawing, or if another one is authentic or not, or find out if we haven't forgotten some collage or other from the same period—and a thousand and one other stupidities like that. Can you imagine? *His* Road to Damascus indeed!"

28 February 1969

Picasso is leafing through a book by a Spanish poet dedicated to painting. The book is profusely illustrated with reproductions, from Piero della Francesca to Pablo Picasso by way

of Veronese and Gutiérrez Solana. Picasso stops turning the pages to look at a magnificent Dürer engraving.

"Amazing," he says. "This is a marvelous engraving. Incredibly enough, many years ago I found a copy of this engraving in a garbage can. In a garbage can, just imagine! Was it in Paris? No, not in Paris. In Gisors, where I had just bought a house. This engraving, in a garbage can!"

While he looks at the Dürer reproduction, completely fascinated, I think that the most incredible part of his story is that he regards the castle in Boisgeloup, so often mentioned in biographies, as just one more house among many. And that one of his first sallies into the neighborhood included rummaging through the trash cans of the region.

The pictures in the book continue to parade before us. Picasso is now looking at a full-color photograph of the Sistine Chapel.

"Well, I was there once. Antonello Trom-

Talking with Rafaël Alberti.

badori [a well-known writer on politics and critic of Italian art] took me to see it. Do you really know it? Now that I think of it, I don't know what's so wonderful about it. It's what I like least of Michelangelo. It's all the same, whether it's the Holy Father or an angel's wing or a slave. Everything is on the same scale and in the same proportion. The truth is, I don't understand it."

He turns the page.

"And this Velázquez? Where did it come from? I've never seen it."

I look in the back pages of the book and find the source.

"From such-and-such a museum."

"I've never seen it. I'm not saying it's false, quite the contrary, just that I don't know it—and it's very lovely."

Given our previous conversation, his comment is cause for a bit of humor—though nothing better than our usual Navas de Malvivir tone:

"With all the respect in the world, Don Hilario, but you are a joker. According to what you said some time ago, you do not like Velázquez at all. Then, to hear you tell it, you have never been in the Prado, nor any other museum in the whole world, except by sheerest accident. However, as soon as a Velázquez shows up—the only Velázquez you don't know!—you shout to the high heavens."

But he is already commenting on another reproduction:

"This *Harlequin* is mine."

Of course it is. Who could deny it? It is none other than the famous 1923 *Harlequin* from the Musée d'Art Moderne in Paris.

"What you don't know, though," he goes on, as if he had guessed my thoughts, "is that the model was named Salvadó—a Catalonian boy, who is still living in Marseilles, I think. He writes sometimes. And you also don't know, nor does almost anybody else, that the Harlequin suit which Salvadó is wearing had been

190

Seated in his favorite chair, Picasso drinks his herb tea after dinner.

given to me by Cocteau."

As on other occasions, he has known just how to respond to my remarks—by telling me to go jump in the lake—but he does it with all the grace in the world.

11 December 1969

As is well known, when Picasso paints he is not "at home" to anyone. A group of Andalusians from Málaga have come to see him today, but they leave without achieving their purpose. That evening, as he comes from his studio, Picasso explains how badly he feels that he was not able to see them:

"What could I do?" he says. "I would have liked to see them—but how? You know, two months ago Jacqueline bought sixty canvases from a paint supplier who was going out of business. Well, there are still eleven canvases unpainted, absolutely blank!"

The people from Málaga have left a gift of a painting, and someone has placed it on a chair.

It is a portrait of a woman with half-closed eyes, her expression vaguely languid and dolorous.

"They said the painter is named Martínez de la Vega and was a great friend of your father's," Picasso's secretary, Miguel, says.

"Of my father's and of mine too," he answers, with his usual insistence on precision. "How can I forget Martínez de la Vega? He was no less than my godfather at my baptism as a painter. He was the one who baptized me at the Círculo Mercantil de Málaga, with a bottle of champagne."

He continues to examine the painting carefully.

"The truth is I'm very sorry not to have seen them. But how could I do it, if there are still eleven canvases to go and the smallest one is the size of this door?"

10 February 1970

We are talking about the painter and his

Working on an engraving.

model. I ask him if it is true that the idea for the painter was Matisse and if it had all come about from seeing a well-known Brassaï photo.

"Nonsense. It's any painter at all, like me, with a model."

"A painter like you? Go on. You've never painted sitting down in your life, nor had a beard, nor a serious studio like the painter in your canvases. Not even a model."

"You're wrong. I had several models. One in particular, a very pretty Japanese girl, who came to the Rue de la Boëtie and made Olga furious. The Japanese girl caused so much trouble that I had to fire her. On the other hand, I never used an easel, or almost never, but who knows—maybe it's because I always wanted to have one."

"But your house is full of easels."

"Not like the one I always wanted. I never found it. That's probably why I paint standing up, or on the floor—I mean, stretching the canvas on the floor and bending down a

thousand times a day. Just imagine! Millions of times a year, at my age. And then there are people who ask me if I ever do any exercise. 'How odd that you should be in such good shape,' they say, 'when you've never done any exercise in your life!' To tell the truth, I don't understand people. For them, exercise probably means riding a bike!"

18 January 1971

There is a white swivel chair in the main room at Notre Dame de Vie with a black cushion on it and a sheepskin spread across the back. It is Picasso's favorite chair and favorite place to be. He spends many hours in it each day, reading newspapers and letters, engraving on copper or signing the etchings which the Crommelynck brothers have brought to the house, or simply chatting with visitors.

Today he is sipping his herb tea and chatting with Rafaël Alberti, who is seated on the other

Picasso seated on the "throne," as the painter jokingly refers to his beloved
armchair, which has accompanied him to each new home for almost fifty years.

side of the table, whiskey in hand. The poet
and the painter have known one another for
almost forty years, and they share a universe of
humor and mischief, a nostalgic and sublime
passion for the bullfight, an Andalusian
childhood, a love of poetry and art, political
exile, and a brotherhood of ideology.

Picasso often speaks of Alberti in terms like
these:

"It's as if he were part of my family. When
he talks to me about his cousins in Cádiz, my
Málaga cousins come to mind. Do you remember the other day he was telling me about an
uncle in Puerto de Santa María, which is near
Cádiz, who bred pigeons in a dovecote he had
built on the terrace of his house? Well, while he
was talking, I kept thinking of an uncle of mine
in Málaga who had built a dovecote on the roof
of *his* house. My uncle had all but moved into
the dovecote. He devoted himself exclusively
to his pigeons. One day he fell off the roof,
with half the dovecote after him, and almost

killed himself. I think he broke a leg and about
twenty ribs."

As on so many other occasions, Picasso and
Alberti are talking about Andalusia, Madrid,
Paris, bulls and bullfighters, poets and paint-
ers, about the days when Picasso was painting
*Guernica,* about the scandal his portrait of
Stalin caused.

Right now the topic of conversation is the
Royal Academy of San Fernando. Picasso
recollects that he went to the famous art school
in Madrid "for one day only," and that the
professors, friends of his father's, naturally
reported back to paternal authority that his
adolescent son was not attending classes.
Alberti recollects his own stay at the same
academy, which lasted two years.

PICASSO: "And who were your professors?"

ALBERTI: "Well, there was Romero de Torres,
who taught dress design, and then I had
Carbonero too. . . ."

PICASSO: "Carbonero? He was a very close

193

In January 1970.

friend of my father's. He came to our house often, every summer, when I was a boy. I'll never forget the hullabaloo which signaled his arrival. A real fiesta! Everyone shouted 'Pepito Carbonero's here, he's come at last,' as if it were the most important event of the year."

A short pause, charged with emotion, keeps Alberti from responding immediately. After a few minutes Picasso comes back to the present and concludes with a typical outburst:

"After all is said and done, I don't know why I think of him with such affection. He was probably one of the professors who reported back to my father about my skipping classes."

19 January 1972

Picasso and Alberti are again carrying on an animated dialogue, in the same room as the year before. They spend a good hour talking and gesturing, listening to one another, and laughing to the point of tears. One could almost say that they are continuing a conversation that they first began in Paris in the early 1930s.

A Spanish lady who is present today manages to interrupt by telling Picasso that she saw Salvador Dalí in Barcelona a short while ago. She speaks rather disparagingly of the Catalonian painter, and Picasso feels obliged to mitigate her sweeping judgments:

"He's a madcap, all right. A regular *tarambana*. He's wonderful."

"A what?" Jacqueline interposes.

"A *tarambana*—what's that in French?"

Alberti and Picasso try unsuccessfully to find a French equivalent for her.

"It's curious," Picasso comments, "but there's really no French word that gives the exact nuance of *tarambana*."

Going back to the subject, Picasso insists that Dalí strikes him as a very sympathetic person:

"You know, he's really quite amusing and nice. An attractive kind of madcap or mad

194

Here begin the last photos that I took of my friend Don Hilario Cuernajon Núñez de Vaca.

hatter or what have you. *Tarambana.* He comes every year to see me and leaves a bouquet of flowers and then disappears."

Alberti is slightly taken aback:

"And do you receive him?"

"Heavens no! How could I? He never steps beyond the outer gate. He just leaves the flowers and disappears."

Perfect understanding and a word to the wise! Alberti, however, belongs to the same generation as Dalí, and is therefore a harsher judge than his friend Picasso:

"Well, he may be an attractive *tarambana* to you, but to my way of thinking he's a *farsante* as well."

"*Farsante?*" Jacqueline asks. Her husband translates the meaning of this word exactly—a fake—while she jots it down in a notebook she keeps precisely for expanding and enriching her vocabulary of Cervantes's language.

Later the Spanish lady returns to the subject of Dalí. Alberti comments rather absently, as if it were scarcely worth bothering to go back to that topic:

"He's not a good painter, but he draws well."

For a second it seems that Picasso is going to add something to Alberti's remark, but then, true to character, he decides against it. Somehow he has always managed, as far as I can remember, not to make a value judgment on the work of other modern artists. He would rather talk about a painter's personality or tell some juicy tidbit about the person in question.

I have often tried to draw him out on the subject of Miró's work, for instance, but have only managed to get him to skim superficially and affectionately over the topic of the celebrated Surrealist painter. Unlike Dalí, he sees Miró every year.

I remember studying the Miró self-portrait in one of the first-floor studios a while back, while Picasso paced about the room, handling this and that, and asking several times:

195

"And what should I show our visitors now to keep them from becoming bored?"

Finding nothing that appealed to him, he joined me in front of the Miró painting and asked me if I knew Miró and how he struck me personally.

"Well, for one thing, he talks less than you do," I told him.

"Naturally, since Miró is a painter and I'm not."

"And what are you?"

"I'm a lot of other things, but people don't take me seriously. They only take me seriously as a painter. Well, that's how it is."

He walked around the easel on which the self-portrait was displayed, crossed his arms, and looked me straight in the eye. As I said nothing, he went on:

"And what do you think of painters like Miró?"

As happens so often, we slipped into schoolboy conversation. The game is to see who can come out on top, by fair means or foul:

"I don't know what to say. A friend of mine—or something I read somewhere—says you compared him to a boy playing with a hoop."

My thrust hits home, and Picasso begins to sputter:

"Not so! Who could have made up such a story? I've been asked about that a thousand times. The truth of the matter is that I don't remember ever saying that, and if I did, it's the same as my calling Rafaël Alberti a failed *picador* turned poet, or saying your sister Enriqueta—her name isn't even Enriqueta—should go to mass more often. What does it all mean? You write it down, leave it, and it ends up printed somewhere. Besides, it would also have to be recorded that Rafaël is not only a failed *picador* but an illegitimate grandson of Louis XVI as well. Because it has to be seen for the madness it is and I'll paint it that way some

"Long will it be before time yields, if ever it does, an Andalusian so bright, so full of adventure." [From the Federico García Lorca poem *Lament for Ignacio Sánchez Mejías.* Translation by Edwin Honig.]

day. Now, if you go and write—or quote me—that Rafaël Alberti is a failed grandson of Louis XVI and, on top of that, leave out all the things leading up to the remark—whether I laughed or winked my eye, whether we left mass together or went to the bullfight—then it's simply better not to put it down on paper. It's the same thing with the story about Miró and the hoop . . ."

And so on, as always, *ad infinitum.*